The
Virtue
Driven
Life

The Virtue Driven Life

Fr. Benedict J. Groeschel, C.F.R.

Our Sunday Visitor Publishing Division
Our Sunday Visitor, Inc.
Huntington, Indiana 46750

Our Sunday Visitor Publishing Division
Our Sunday Visitor, Inc.
200 Noll Plaza
Huntington, IN 46750

ISBN-13: 978-1-59276-265-1
ISBN-10: 1-59276-265-4 (Inventory No. T320)
LCCN: 2006932354

Cover design by Tyler Ottinger
Cover art courtesy of The Crosiers
Interior design by Sherri L. Hoffman

PRINTED IN THE UNITED STATES OF AMERICA

This book is dedicated
to Pope Benedict XVI
with great personal and prayerful regard.

Contents

Introduction

*V*IRTUE HAS BECOME a forgotten word. Today if someone says to you, "Oh, she's very virtuous," it is not likely to be seen as a compliment. The word conveys to many people an image of someone who is "soft and fuzzy" or "tough and prickly." *Virtuous* is often used in a sarcastic, cynical way by those who have no regard for virtue themselves and criticize it in others. This is a frequent phenomenon in the pages of newspapers and various other organs of public confusion, which, out of the morass of moral relativism, oddly set themselves up as the moral judges of the world. This reminds me of Yuri Andropov, who succeeded Leonid Brezhnev as premier of the Soviet Union. For several years Andropov had been director of the KGB, the Soviet secret police — hardly a position known for great virtue. I remember that he once accused somebody else's foreign policy — it may have been ours — of being insincere.[1] How little we know ourselves.

Virtue, therefore, is a very odd word in our world, and we don't get much help from many theologians today. In fact, they are something of a hindrance. Some theologians have recently embraced the idea that virtue is nothing really significant, just a trait of behavior.[2] In fact, the philosophers and, recently, some of the psychologists are much more help.

Certain behaviors are often considered good traits: friendliness and even-temperedness, for example. Traits that are pleasant or helpful we tend to call *virtues*. This misses the whole point. This is, in fact, the view of the experimental psychologists, who look at human beings as complicated animals. Experimental psychologists study pigeons or white rats or even glowworms to figure out what people are going to do. If you take that worm's-eye view of human nature, you would just say that virtues are series of behaviors that we have decided to identify as good. And since we don't know what goodness means, we might say "nice."

According to these people, virtues are neither good nor bad. This notion of virtue would ultimately have to be traced back to a philosopher whose name we all know. We seldom realize, however, the damage this well-meaning person caused. He's living proof that kindly, virtuous people can do all kinds of damage. Immanuel Kant, relying on pure reason, sought to avoid giving values to things, at least in his most influential work. You may think that one thing is good; another person may think something else is good. Nobody's right and nobody's wrong. Kant, fortunately, did not live by this theory, because he was a devout Christian.[3] He seemed a pious old man who was neutral about everything except his own life, which was virtuous. But Kant's interpretation of the process of knowing is a dangerous point of view. It took into account neither right nor wrong.

Humans vs. Animals

WHEN I WAS STUDYING cognitive science at Columbia University, I decided to do an exercise in academic freedom. I argued with my professors on a very limited view of human nature made popular in our time by the famous experimental psychologist B. F. Skinner. His teaching incorporated a view of human nature that represented a school of psychology called *behavior-*

ism. It included MacDougal, Guthrie, Hall, Clark, Watson, and Skinner — all of which are Scottish names. These men were raised in the Scottish Calvinist tradition, which firmly denied free will. Having given up their Presbyterian affiliations, they then decided that people were complicated animals. Before his death, Skinner admitted that he was really not an atheist but had pretended to be an atheist because he didn't know what to do with God. He eventually seemed to return to the view of the radical Calvinism of his youth. In his autobiography, as well as in a popular article in *Psychology Today*, he refers to three of the four Gospels (see, for example, Luke 17:33). He pointed out that it may strike some people as strange that the idea of gaining one's life vs. losing one's life "should be, as I think it is, the central theme of a behavioral science."[4] He never gave up a behavioristic point of view. He still thought of people as complicated pigeons. He wrote a book called *Beyond Freedom and Dignity*, denying that human beings really had either one.

Probably the most radical of all of these behaviorists was Edwin Guthrie. I never knew anything about his personal life, but he must have been unusual. Guthrie described human beings as a torus. A torus is a doughnut, a round thing that has a surface on all sides. Human beings were tori. I'll leave you to think of the biology of this idea. According to Guthrie, a human being is a torus, on the surface of which are receptors for stimuli. Life is just a series of responses to these stimuli. This is a somewhat narrow view of human nature! It is really a description of a paramecium, a little creature that simply crawls around and looks for things to eat. The idea of a torus does not do justice even to pet dogs and cats — or even birds for that matter.

Although it was useful in experimental psychology, the behavioristic point of view has been very destructive in modern life, and many acute moral issues facing the human race are based precisely on this view of human beings as complicated animals. When animals get too complicated and are not cooperative, what do we do? We put them to sleep. A man who falsely claimed to be very virtuous, who sought to create a nation of virtuous people according to his definition of virtue — a super race — gassed millions of people to accomplish his goal. I have walked through the gas chambers at Auschwitz, where almost a million people were put to death because they did not fit his idea of virtue.

What does this have to do with Holy Scripture? Holy Scripture takes a very different view of man, as, for example, in Psalm 1, known in Latin as *Beatus vir*:

> Blessed is the man
> who walks not in the counsel of the wicked,
> nor stands in the way of sinners,
>> nor sits in the seat of scoffers;
> but his delight is in the law of the LORD,
>> and on his law he meditates day and night.
> He is like a tree
>> planted by streams of water
> that yields its fruit in its season,
>> and its leaf does not wither.
> In all that he does, he prospers. (Psalm 1:1–3)

I would say the psalmist has a clear idea of goodness, of virtue of the blessed man. And he has an idea of the unblessed man:

> The wicked are not so,
>> but are like chaff which the wind drives away.
> Therefore the wicked will not stand in the judgment,

nor sinners in the congregation of the righteous;
for the LORD knows the way of the righteous,
but the way of the wicked will perish (Psalm 1:4–6).

If we look for virtue in the teachings of our Lord Jesus Christ, we are flooded with texts. Perhaps it would be helpful at this point for readers to meditate on the Sermon on the Mount (Matthew 5–7).

It is obvious that Sacred Scripture and religious books of other traditions call for a life of virtue. In contemporary jargon, however, the good man makes *value judgments*. This means that some of us white mice like to do this and other white mice like to do that, and we call it virtue. I would much rather my idea of goodness be based on the Psalms and the Sermon on the Mount.

A Revolution in Psychology: Virtue Comes Back

THE MORAL PHILOSOPHERS of ancient times, especially the Greeks, and the Church Fathers and mystics were the first students of the mind; in fact, they were the first psychologists. They were all interested in virtue, qualities of the human personality that moved people toward consistently good behavior, toward the "good life." They were also interested in character strengths like loyalty and perseverance, which are components of a virtuous life. Then in the nineteenth century came *behaviorism*, with its denial of insight and dignity; its close companion was *determinism*, with its denial of virtue and freedom. This leads to something oddly called *moral positivism*, a theory that sees what most people think and do as right. *Positivism* is presumably that which does not need proof.

The immense influence of popular (pop) psychology led many to deny the existence of character and virtue, or to substitute for them something called *values clarification*. This was a ritual for determining what people really wanted and getting them to recognize the contradictions inherent in their goals. Naturally, because virtue is always there, people often wove into values clarification various virtues, but they could not be identified as such. What has emerged is a group of people who are like a fleet of ships without rudders, compasses, or maps — or, better still, like a city without foundations.

However, more humanistic theories about human nature began to emerge — ideas related to free will, meaning, human relationships, culture, affirmation, and the recognition of the autonomous self.[5] Theorists with explicit religious and moral values, like Father Adrian van Kaam and Gerald May, also began to be read. Then a powerful voice for self-understanding, coupled with common sense, was raised, and Aaron Beck introduced *cognitive psychology* into therapy. This opened the door wider for concepts like freedom, personal responsibility, and even religious values. The idea that we are not merely a collection of our thoughts and impulses, that the individual may direct his or her thinking and behavior, seems obvious to many people, but actually Beck was a pioneer of the obvious that had been forgotten.

Finally, by a logical historical process, positive psychology came into existence, led by Martin Seligman, a former president of the American Psychological Association, and Christopher Peterson. They were joined by many others who began to embrace a positive psychology that was focused on human strengths rather than on weakness and pathology. Paul Vitz, in a most enlightening article addressed to readers who are not professional psychologists, sums up this important development. After evaluating negative psychology, he writes:

What is needed to balance our understanding of the person is a recognition of positive human characteristics that can both heal many of our pathologies and help to prevent psychological problems in one's future life. Positive psychology therefore emphasizes traits that promote happiness and well-being, as well as character strengths such as optimism, kindness, resilience, persistence, and gratitude. These positive characteristics, sometimes called "character strengths" or even "ego strengths" by psychologists, will be recognized by members of all major religions and by most philosophers as names for what used to be called "the virtues."[6]

Vitz praises Peterson and Seligman, who invite psychology to "reclaim the study of character and virtue as legitimate topics of psychological inquiry and informed societal discourse. By providing ways of talking about character strengths and measuring them across the life span, this . . . will start to make possible a science of human strengths that goes beyond armchair philosophy and political rhetoric. We believe that good character can be cultivated, but to do so, we need conceptual and empirical tools to craft and evaluate interventions."[7]

Of course, this new insight introduces new terminology. How do we define *virtue*? Peterson and Seligman write that virtues "are the core characteristics valued by moral philosophers and religious thinkers: wisdom, courage, humanity, justice, temperance, and transcendence."

They give historical surveys of these virtues. Character strengths "are the psychological ingredients — processes or mechanisms — that define the virtues. . . . [T]hey are distinguishable routes to displaying one or another of the virtues. For example, the virtue of wisdom can be achieved through such strengths as creativity, curiosity, love of learning, open-mindedness, and what we call perspective — having a 'big picture' on life."[8]

Although we are using the classical list of four moral virtues and three theological virtues — not quite the same list used by Professors Peterson and Seligman — we are covering the same material. Our approach is more classical and perhaps easier for the average reader to deal with, especially for readers familiar with authoritative writings on the spiritual life. Those particularly interested in moral theology, ethics, or serious approaches to education, child rearing, and character development would do very well to review their landmark book carefully.

What Is a Virtue?

THIS IS AN INTERESTING QUESTION, although not very practical. There have been millions of virtuous people who could not even think of defining virtue. Positive psychology bases its definition on what might be called a canvassing of recognized moral and religious figures, sages, and saints. This gave the positive psychologists a good start. They indicated the character strengths that make up a virtuous disposition. Peterson and Seligman and their associates do this with great care and creativity. One must ask: Is there something more? Dietrich von Hildebrand, who carefully pondered this question, defined virtue as a quality of someone's character.[9] The virtue is present even when it is not operative or actualized. (He refers to this as being "superactualized.") For example, a chaste person is chaste even when asleep. I would go even further and say that the person is chaste even if sleep brings sexual dreams containing images that would be unchaste if they were welcomed in times of watchful responsibility. Virtues go beyond present thinking. A patient person who becomes unexpectedly impatient for a moment will quickly return to the customary patient disposition when the situation has passed. I say this as someone who has experienced the mild impatience of two or three people who are likely to be canonized one day as saints and who were generally patient to a heroic degree. We have only to think of various testy passages in the Pauline epistles to see how a saintly person may for a moment become impatient.

Virtue, therefore, is more than a series of good deeds. It exists in a person's depths. Presumably, there must be some neurological component because we are made up of body, soul, and spirit. However, I think there is something beyond the physical, not perceptible to scientific comprehension — an aspect of virtue that rises from the depth of the soul. Psychology, understood as a science or as philosophy, cannot deal directly with this mysterious aspect of virtue, which in turn is part of a greater mysterious reality that we call *the human being*.

Natural (Human) Virtues

GOOD TRAITS, OR VIRTUES, can exist in a number of ways. First of all, there are the naturally decent people. We may not know a thing about them — whether they believe or disbelieve, whether they pray or they don't pray. Or perhaps we know that they do not believe or pray, but they are honest and kind. They are willing to speak up at the right moment, are respectful of their neighbors' rights and needs, and do not lead an indulgent life. They have what is called *natural virtue*, which can coexist with a lot of other things that are not so naturally virtuous.[10] Naturally virtuous people, like supernaturally virtuous people, can have lots of faults and sins, and they fail here and there. Basically, they seem to be pretty good people, but you do not expect them to be perfect.

I have a friend who identifies himself as a retired Euro-communist, which means he is a communist with a swimming pool in his backyard. Definitely very upper-middle class, he was nevertheless sympathetic to the more humane communist causes until the collapse of communism. Disclosures from the former Soviet Union revealed that those who presented themselves as the benevolent benefactors of mankind could be quite as ruthless and bloody as the Nazis. Current or former communist sympathizers often conveniently forget that the Bolsheviks and the Nazis were military allies for a couple of years.

My Eurocommunist friend would profoundly despise the murderous actions of the Bolsheviks. He is a decent and generous man. His son became a devout Catholic, although he had no Catholic influences at all. I pray for my friend, who is a physician and a naturally virtuous person. On the other hand, I know people who have some supernatural values but are nowhere near as decent as this man. They operate on something else. They may have faith, but with regard to virtue they are doing a lot worse. Our Lord told us that not everyone who says to Him, "Lord, Lord," will enter the kingdom of heaven (Matthew 7:21). Some believers do not do very well living up to their beliefs. Remember the admonition of Saint James: "You believe that God is one; you do well. Even the demons believe — and shudder" (James 2:19). Saint Peter's second epistle recognizes that faith requires virtuous acts:

> For this very reason make every effort to supplement
> your faith with virtue, and virtue with knowledge, and
> knowledge with self-control, and self-control with

steadfastness, and steadfastness with godliness, and godliness with brotherly affection, and brotherly affection with love. (2 Peter 1:5–7)

So, natural virtues are good, decent qualities that are often passed on by environment, especially by the home. We know very well the importance of care, love, concern, and good example in the raising of children. Some traits may be passed on by genetic inheritance — qualities like even-temperedness — that are consistent with virtues.

Therefore, natural virtue is a good thing. In his great book *The City of God*, Saint Augustine praises the natural virtue of the ancient Romans who established the Roman city-state, right up to the time of Julius Caesar. Augustine said that the empire was falling apart in his time (the barbarian chieftain Alaric had sacked Rome in 410) because the Romans had given up natural virtue. It is all too obvious today that Western European countries are busy undermining the foundations of natural virtue in their own societies. For example, the widespread use of pornography undermines any natural dignity and regard for the human rights of those who are represented only as objects of lust. The United States is not far behind Europe.

An Important Distinction

IT IS UNFORTUNATE that the *Catechism of the Catholic Church* does not sufficiently distinguish between natural (human) and supernatural moral virtues, which is a classical distinction made by Saint Thomas Aquinas and many other authors. Although all virtues call us to do good, those that are the result of grace and lead to a holy life need to be distinguished from natural virtues or simply good human qualities. These supernatural virtues, which are an expression of grace, are sometimes called *infused moral virtues*, indicating that they rely on the grace of Christ won by our Savior on the Cross. Wherever they exist, they depend on His grace.[11]

Supernatural Moral Virtue

BEYOND NATURAL, OR HUMAN, virtue there are *supernatural moral virtues* — that is, good qualities and character strengths of the natural sort raised to the supernatural order by the mysterious reality called *grace*, which strengthens good qualities, makes them more consistent, and changes their goal or motivation. Why, for example, is someone prudent or just? If you know why somebody is doing something, that will explain why they do it in a certain way and why they do it even when they are under great pressure not to be virtuous. The ultimate goal of mature Christian virtue is to please God and to come at last to His embrace in eternal life. The goal of natural virtues is to lead a good life in this world.

There are many lists of virtues. The shortest and most comprehensive list comes from the Greek and Roman philosophers — but it would also be acceptable to Chinese and Oriental philosophers — and would include prudence, justice, fortitude, and temperance. These are called *cardinal, or pivotal, virtues*. Contemporary writers on positive psychology add two other categories: humanity and transcendence. These two open the door to some consideration of the theological virtues of faith, hope, and charity. However, since these writers cannot and do not make an assumption of the Christian faith, they cannot really describe the qualities related to transcendence in terms of the supernatural. They merely offer the possibility of considering qualities of humanity that extend beyond what human relationships demand.

They also offer the possibility of the human relationship with the divine, which of course depends on revelation.

From prudence, justice, fortitude, and temperance come many other virtues: benevolence, kindliness, chastity, honesty, a certain courage in the face of life, and stick-to-itiveness. There are all kinds of good qualities in human nature that can be raised to the order of the supernatural, like justice and kindness. However, the supernatural virtues always include as their first motive the desire to please God and to do His will.

One of the natural virtues is the virtue of religion (not the virtue of faith), which we will examine later. William Bennett in his *Book of Virtues* makes a little mistake — on purpose, I suspect, so that people will understand what he is trying to say. *The Book of Virtues* is about the first four virtues and their different departments, and at the end he places the virtue of faith. But when we read it, we realize that he means the virtue of religion. The virtue of religion is a good quality that makes decent human beings worship their Creator and try to fulfill His laws as they understand them. For this reason no society is without religion.

Enver Hoxha, the brutal communist dictator of Albania, now gone to his eternal judgment, bragged that he had the only totally nonreligious country in the world. He was kidding himself. No sooner had his yoke been taken away than religion resurfaced, and my good friend, Father Rock Mirdita, pastor of the Albanian Catholic church in Scarsdale, New York, was ordained archbishop of Tirana and primate of Albania by Pope John Paul II in Albania, in the presence of Mother Teresa, Albania's most famous citizen ever. So much for Mr. Hoxha and imposed atheism.

If the seventy years of Bolshevik persecution of religion have proved anything, it is that religion buries its undertakers, and it does not seem to make much difference whether the militant atheists have attacked Christians, Muslims, Buddhists, Hindus, or anyone else. They will all be there at the funeral because the virtue of religion is part of human nature.[12]

Peterson and Seligman, struggling to be as general and objective as possible, and using terms like religion and faith, put all religious actions under the name of transcendence. They understandably stick with a largely sociological description of faith, which in this context means works or actions inspired or directed by faith. They do not attempt to explore the content of faith, leaving that to theologians, spiritual writers, and others.

Time magazine reported a few years ago that 94 percent of Americans pray and believe that their prayers are answered. Don't assume that that is faith. That could be the natural virtue of religion, for which we are grateful. The European Values Study twenty years ago revealed that 6 percent of the atheists in Ireland believe in the divinity of Christ. (The Irish can be very complicated when it comes to matters of religion.) Consider James Joyce and Samuel Beckett, both of whom were identified as Irish atheists. After preaching nihilism and meaninglessness for years, Beckett in his old age was quoted as saying, "Please God" and "God bless." "God bless" is a devout Irish way of saying good-bye. Nikita Khrushchev once said, "Next year I will go to Washington, God willing." Even American atheists will somberly sit at a meeting of the League of the Militant Godless, and when somebody sneezes, they will all say, "God bless you." Nature will simply not let us escape from God.

Theological Virtues

WE MUST ALSO LOOK at the theological virtues. They are the kind of virtues that go beyond any natural human experience. They are faith, hope, and charity.

You may say, "I believe in the American way of life and in God, the Father Almighty." If you believe in both the same way, your belief in God stems from the natural virtue of religion. The theological virtue of faith is completely different. If someone says to me, "I generally accept the teachings of the Church, but I don't accept this one because I don't understand it," they are showing a lack of faith. They are talking as if their problem is with the virtue of religion and are not even aware of their problem with faith. We can have degrees of faith. The apostles said to the Lord, "Increase our faith." Our Lord says, "Oh, you of little faith," so we can have more or less. If we disagree with Church teachings in one or more areas, do we realize we are going against the faith of all those in the past: apostles, martyrs, Church Fathers, popes? Do we want to disagree with all those people on a matter that may pertain to our salvation? It is worth thinking about.

I once preached at a Unitarian Church on what Catholics and Unitarians have in common. It was a short sermon. I accepted the invitation to preach because the minister told me half the congregation were ex-Catholics. I said to the minister before I began, "What is the theological climate here?" He answered, "Well, they're about 75 percent agnostic and 25 percent atheist."

"What a mysterious religion," I thought. What a mysterious religion! Why would anyone get out of bed on a Sunday morning if they do not believe in God? The answer lies in the natural virtue of religion, not in the theological virtue of faith.

We are going to consider in these chapters the natural virtues and then the same virtues lifted by grace to a supernatural level, which I will refer to as supernatural, or Christian, moral virtues. Psychology has insisted for years that a human being is impelled to relive the past in response to biology and inheritance. This kind of psychology is generally called *clinical* — an adjective meaning "bedside" — because the focus was on getting rid of pathology, or sickness, rooted in the past. As we have noted, the attention of psychology is moving toward a more positive view of human nature, toward strengths of character, good values, and virtues. We are no longer focused exclusively on a life driven by need or illness. What we are looking for is a life motivated and moved by forces for good — that is, a virtuous life.

Then we will look at the theological virtues of faith, hope, and charity; they are called *theological* because they are gifts from God alone. They are quite different from the supernatural moral virtues in origin and object. As we will see, they bring the mysterious and intangible into human experience. In his illuminating book *Introduction to Christianity*, Pope Benedict XVI reminds us that when we are dealing with the gifts of the God of Abraham, Isaac, and Jacob, the Father of our Lord Jesus Christ, we are beyond what is visible and comprehensible to our minds.[13] We are on the threshold of what Einstein meant when he referred to "the highest wisdom and the most radiant beauty that our dull faculties can comprehend." It can be said in a carefully qualified way that the new psychology is pointing in the right direction and to important things. We need to be careful to acknowledge that faith, hope, and charity go beyond all that nature, even at its best, can provide to humans on the journey to an incomprehensible eternity.

The Christian on this road must be impelled by the virtues the philosophers recognize and by the supernatural virtues that are these same qualities raised and ennobled by grace. Saint Paul, the great psychologist, says that faith, hope, and love are the things that bring us to salvation won for us by Christ on the Cross. If we truly seek these, we will lead a virtuous life.

PART I

The Cardinal Virtues

Prudence

Justice

Fortitude

Temperance

Human Natural Virtues

"Whatever is true, whatever is honorable, whatever is just, whatever is pure, whatever is lovely, whatever is gracious, if there is any excellence, if there is anything worthy of praise, think about these things" (Philippians 4:8).

A virtue is a habitual and firm disposition to do the good. It allows the person not only to perform good acts, but to give the best of himself. The virtuous person tends toward the good with all his sensory and spiritual powers; he pursues the good and chooses it in concrete actions.

— CATECHISM OF THE CATHOLIC CHURCH (N. 1803)

Human virtues *are firm attitudes, stable dispositions, habitual perfections of intellect and will that govern our actions, order our passions, and guide our conduct according to reason and faith. They make possible ease, self-mastery, and joy in leading a morally good life. The virtuous man is he who freely practices the good.*

The moral virtues are acquired by human effort. They are the fruit and seed of morally good acts; they dispose all the powers of the human being for communion with divine love.

— CATECHISM OF THE CATHOLIC CHURCH (N. 1804)

Human virtues *acquired by education, by deliberate acts and by a perseverance ever-renewed in repeated efforts are purified and elevated by divine grace. With God's help, they forge character and give facility in the practice of the good. The virtuous man is happy to practice them.*

— CATECHISM OF THE CATHOLIC CHURCH (N. 1810)

Supernatural Moral Virtues

It is not easy for man, wounded by sin, to maintain moral balance. Christ's gift of salvation offers us the grace necessary to persevere in the pursuit of the virtues. Everyone should always ask for this grace of light and strength, frequent the sacraments, cooperate with the Holy Spirit, and follow his calls to love what is good and shun evil.

— CATECHISM OF THE CATHOLIC CHURCH (N. 1811)

"To live well is nothing other than to love God with all one's heart, with all one's soul and with all one's efforts; from this it comes about that love is kept whole and uncorrupted (through temperance). No misfortune can disturb it (and this is fortitude). It obeys only [God] (and this is justice), and is careful in discerning things, so as not to be surprised by deceit or trickery (and this is prudence)." — Saint Augustine[14]

— CATECHISM OF THE CATHOLIC CHURCH (N. 1809)

CHAPTER 1

Prudence

O simple ones, learn prudence; O foolish men, pay attention.

— PROVERBS 8:5

Prudence *is the virtue that disposes practical reason to discern our true good in every circumstance and to choose the right means of achieving it; "the prudent man looks where he is going" (Proverbs 14:15). . . . Prudence is "right reason in action," writes St. Thomas Aquinas. . . .*[15] *[It] guides the other virtues by setting rule and measure. It is prudence that immediately guides the judgment of conscience. The prudent man determines and directs his conduct in accordance with this judgment. With the help of this virtue we apply moral principles to particular cases without error and overcome doubts about the good to achieve and the evil to avoid.*

— CATECHISM OF THE CATHOLIC CHURCH (N. 1806)

DOES ANY VIRTUE have a worse name than prudence? Perhaps temperance. Years ago some Protestant girls used to be named Prudy, or Prudence. (Catholic girls used to be named for saints.) It was a tough thing to live down, and I suspect that most of them have changed their names. The natural virtue of prudence assists people to organize their lives and activities in order to achieve the goal of a happy life in this world.

The founders of the United States, being realists, did not say everybody had a right to life, liberty, and happiness; they maintained that everybody had a right to life, liberty, and *the pursuit of* happiness, or trying to be happy. Prudence tells us how to pursue happiness. It makes us organize things so that we can be happy according to whatever our definition of happiness is. Often, unfortunately, the definition of happiness is provided by advertising and the media. One advertisement showed a couple standing on the edge of the Grand Canyon. How did they get there? "Money." Money, it was implied, brings happiness. It does not. Money brings comfort and, in this case, travel.

Those of us who grew up as children or grandchildren of immigrants knew very clearly what was going to bring us happiness. If you lived in lower Manhattan, happiness would come if you moved to upper Manhattan: Inwood or Washington Heights. If you lived in the South Bronx, you would be happy if you made it out of the city to Mount Vernon or Yonkers. The next generation would be happy if they made it to affluent Scarsdale or Bronxville. The next generation tried to make it to posh South Salem. It depended on one's perspective. Attitudes like this were plainly summed up by Samuel Gompers, a leader in the early labor movement. One time an American president said to Samuel, "What do the unions want, Sam?" And he responded, "More."

We think more will make us happy. By the time we get about three generations out of the South Bronx or Jersey City, we know it isn't true. When I was a little boy in Jersey City, my father said in our own native idiom, "If we don't do another thing, we're going to get the hell out of Jersey City." Happiness was to be found in suburban Essex County. The promised land. So we moved to the suburbs. Life was more pleasant but less interesting than it was in the city. And it still had its difficulties and sorrows.

Once when I was in Florida, I heard someone on the radio say, "Come to Certainty Village, the retirement home of your dreams. Everything you ever wanted." The pitch went on to describe a number of things I never even thought of wanting: an eighteen-hole golf course, a sauna, a masseuse every day. I didn't want any of these things. "Everything you ever wanted" — while you wait for the undertaker.

Look at your own life and how you set things up prudently. A certain amount of natural prudence or common sense is good. Did you ever meet someone who hasn't got the brains to come in out of the rain? Such people are imprudent. They take wild chances. Most of them are failures, but some are successful — self-made men, even billionaires. But they are always in danger because, having been fortunate in one circumstance, they continue to be imprudent and often eventually come to ruin.

> **Look at your own life and how you set things up prudently.**

The Christian Moral Virtue of Prudence

THE SUPERNATURAL VIRTUE of prudence makes us organize our activities, desires, possibilities, resources, and behavior in such a way that we may come to eternal life. We can do many things that are imprudent from a worldly perspective but which are prudent for eternal life. Saint Paul says that "the foolishness of God is wiser than men" (1 Corinthians 1:25).

Even very religious people are often conflicted about whether to follow the natural virtue of prudence or prudence aimed at eternal life. The circumstances of human existence often call for a delicate balance between the two.

We must have natural prudence. If a garage mechanic says, "If you don't get this car serviced every three thousand miles, you're in trouble," you should get the car serviced. Don't be naturally imprudent for the honor and glory of God unless natural prudence and supernatural wisdom clash. The only time you can be naturally imprudent for the honor and glory of God is when the supernatural virtue of prudence contradicts the natural.

I will use several examples drawn from the conflict between the Nazi Party and the Catholic Church to illustrate different kinds of prudence.

The number of Jewish people saved by Pope Pius XII is hard to estimate. Many say that he saved more Jews than any other single person.[16] In most countries of Europe, 85 percent of the Jewish population perished under Hitler. In two countries that was not true: Denmark and Italy. In both countries, only 15 percent of the Jewish population perished, which is still horrible, but it was an improvement over the other. Thousands of Jewish people were hidden in the city of Rome — in convents, in monasteries, in the Vatican, which was so crowded that the Pope gave the refugees his own rooms in his summer residence. Pope Pius XII constantly called for an end to the persecution of people because of their race or religion. He condemned the persecution relentlessly, not mentioning names, and pleaded for an end to genocide in his Christmas message of 1942.

Who was he talking about? Obviously the victims were Jews and gypsies. In January 1943 a letter appeared in the *New York Times*, praising the Catholic Church and the Pope as the only voices raised in defense of Jews in Europe, and it was signed by Albert Einstein. I have a copy of the letter.[17]

At times Pope Pius XII thought seriously of directly confronting the Nazis by name, in which case he knew he would be kidnapped, held incommunicado, taken to Germany, and perhaps used as a hostage. The Nazis were quite capable of sending out messages with his name on them. In fact, it is believed that he left instructions that if he were arrested, no messages of his were to be taken seriously.

Pope Pius XII decided not to condemn the Nazis directly and openly by name, and so he is now viciously attacked. The bishops of Holland, on the other hand, openly attacked the Nazi occupation forces for the transportation of Jewish people to Eastern Europe and to death. Immediately, Arthur Seyss-Inquart, the Nazi high commissioner in Holland, ordered the arrest and deportation of all Jews who had become Christian and all people of partial Jewish origin. Many died as a result, including Saint Teresa Benedicta of the Cross (Edith Stein) and her sister Rosa. Who was prudent and who was imprudent? I leave that to others to decide, but I would fiercely defend the intentions of Pope Pius. At the end of World War II, the chief rabbi of Rome, Eugenio Zolli, became a Catholic. He took Eugenio as his Christian name in order to honor Pope Pius XII (Eugenio Pacelli).

In 1938, the Nazis held a plebiscite in Germany. Five hundred thousand votes were cast against Hitler, out of millions of votes. Most of those who voted against him — in an open ballot — had been members of the Catholic Party in Germany, which after the war became the Christian Democratic Party. The Carmelite nuns in Cologne did not know what to do, because the ballot was not secret. Hitler had closed many religious houses and evicted the religious. Friends told the sisters, "Vote for Hitler because it's not going to make any difference anyway." The sisters decided that they would probably not vote, which was also dangerous. Sister Teresa Benedicta (Edith Stein), who was a Jew and a nun of the Cologne Carmel, said, "Under no circumstances can you vote for Hitler. He is doing the work of Satan. He is the enemy of Christ, and he will bring our country to ruin." When the election committee arrived at the monastery, the head of the committee noticed that not all the sisters were voting. As he called off one of the names, the superior said, "Well, that sister is very aged and infirm and not capable of voting."

"What about Dr. Edith Stein?" he asked.

"She has no vote" was the answer.

"Why? She's old enough to vote."

"She's not Aryan," the superior replied, indicating that she was Jewish.

From that moment on, Sister Teresa Benedicta was on her way to the gas chambers, but she was also on the way to canonization as a martyr. Her name has lived on long after her tormentors have been forgotten. She did not renounce her vows and abandon her vocation to Carmel. Before her arrest she could have tried to flee secretly, but she chose to remain and allow God to direct her life. This is the difference between natural and supernatural prudence as far as their effects are concerned.

Prudence in America

IN AMERICA, we like to deceive ourselves into thinking that no dangerous decisions will be made in public policy. Two Catholic candidates were running for Congress; one was pro-life and the other was pro-abortion. The pro-life candidate lost by one quarter of one percent, but he did not get any kind of real support from Church authorities. I don't say that the

Church should support candidates, but it should make clear that you place your eternal salvation in jeopardy if you support those who take human life. If Church leaders do not say that, they are remiss in fulfilling their apostolic mandate. You can vote for anyone you like, but think carefully before voting for someone who takes his salvation into his hands. Don't join him.

We are involved in no small conflict. Our present debates are moving toward the Hitlerian question of life unworthy of life. Think of the immense imprudence of the people whose pictures I saw at Auschwitz. Many of them had opposed the Nazis one way or another. These were not Jews, because Jewish people were not even photographed when they went to Auschwitz. They were dead in a few hours. The victims whose photos are there had imprudently offended the Nazis, but they had been witnesses to the truth with divine prudence.

Human prudence is not divine prudence. There are innumerable stories from times of persecution and tyranny that illustrate the difference between prudence of the flesh and prudence of the spirit. There are many examples of the conflict between natural and supernatural prudence.

I was very active in the early days of the civil rights movement despite warnings that I might alienate some of my friends. I have never regretted a minute of my involvement. I saw the movement change in the course of time and become a number of other movements, some of which I did not agree with, but essentially it was a holy movement. Here was an incredible and outrageous injustice that had gone on for centuries. I realized that it was even more dangerous to do nothing against this evil. I used to hear this saying: "They came for the gypsies, and nobody said anything. They came for the black people, and nobody said anything. They came for the

Jews, and nobody said anything. And they came for me, and nobody said anything."

In Auschwitz, the most professional exhibit is sponsored by a Jewish organization. At the end of seeing the exhibit, you're sick. The last set of pictures, the last gallery of the exhibit, is about those who tried to help the Jews. There's a picture of a Polish priest in his vestments with all the altar boys of the old style. He was killed trying to assist Jews to escape. In the monastery that Saint Maximilian Kolbe founded, the friars accepted three thousand refugees. It was the largest Catholic monastery in the world when the Russians invaded from the east. Then the Nazis came. One thousand of those refugees were Jewish. There was no place for them to stay, so almost all of the refugees — some three thousand — were parceled out in the neighboring villages and towns. But a number of Jewish men remained hidden at Niepokalanow, the Monastery of Our Lady, wearing friars' habits. Gradually, they were rounded up, as the friars were. Most of the friars died or were killed in Auschwitz. I was told that one Jewish man survived until 1944, hidden in the monastery, where he was finally captured. The friars had certainly acted against all human prudence, but they did what they were supposed to do as Christians and men of God.

> **Confrontational events can force us to ask the question: Do I put supernatural prudence before the natural? Do I put my eternal salvation and that of others first?**

Confrontational events can force us to ask the question: Do I put supernatural prudence before the natural? Do I put my eternal salvation and that of others first? I have to say that many times in my life I have not. I put other things first: convenience, comfort, pleasantness, acceptance, human respect, ambition, what people thought of me. Maybe you have never been in a situation where people were openly hostile to your religious values. Maybe you've never been called names in public by unknown strangers. Maybe you've never been spit at, vilified. I suggest that it would not be bad to have such an experience. It does marvels for your soul. Let people curse or swear at you. After a couple of times, you don't even give a hoot. But we're so afraid of any kind of confrontation that natural prudence calls us to silence when we should speak up.

In the twentieth century, Christians unfortunately failed to speak up a number of times. Perhaps this is not surprising, because they were not used to being attacked. The Gospel and the Church try to remind us that we have to use supernatural prudence and courage (another virtue we will discuss) when we are faced with evil. The Church celebrates the martyrs so that we will recognize the need to suffer for the truth. The Second World War and the communist persecution present many examples of those who did naturally imprudent things in order to seek their salvation and that of their enemies.

I have seen pictures of the Polish Sisters of the Holy Family of Nazareth in their habits, kneeling by the edge of a trench, into which they were to be dumped after they were shot. How do people shoot nuns in habits? How do they shoot little children? Where do you find people to do this? You don't find them. You make them. It's very simple. All you have to do is intimidate people and then convince them that the others are not human. I have talked to priests who had been prisoners at Auschwitz, and they told me, "We were treated like animals by people who hated animals."

On the anniversary of the founding of the Nazi Party and on Hitler's birthday, ten Catholic priests were shot in every camp in honor of the event. To celebrate his birthday! How did these madmen ever get in charge? Those who should have opposed the Nazis were too prudent with an earthly prudence that now seems like cowardice. I think we are very imprudent in our society. Supernaturally imprudent.

We have examples of this kind of apparent prudence, which is even naturally imprudent in the United States. Twenty years ago, on gay rights day in New York, the police were not allowed to do anything. They were ordered to have no incidents. Protesters walked stark naked in front of Saint Patrick's Cathedral. They made obscene gestures on Fifth Avenue, in front of the cathedral. The man who was then mayor attended part of the day's events, the so-called gay games. He welcomed the gay community to New York, and he was certainly free to do that. But were those who violated that law that day not subject to it like everybody else?

When a Mass at Saint Patrick's Cathedral was interrupted by ACT UP and various militant abortion organizations, the police were very upset. They were furious because they were told "hands off." Finally a loud ruckus began at the Mass, and they cleared the protesters from the cathedral in eight minutes. The protesters had gone too far. A man with tears in his eyes came up to me after the Mass and said, "You know, as bad as they were, the Bolsheviks never interrupted a Mass." The strangest thing was that the demonstrators that day claimed, and really thought, that they were going to get more respect and understanding for the gay community. This judgment was not prudent in any sense of the word.

I have never in my life thought of insulting anyone because of sexual orientation. I have often tried to win understanding and sympathy for people who carry the burden of sexual identity conflict. I would no more think of offending them than I would think of offending someone who is old or bald or albino or who speaks with an accent. My mother taught me better than that. But I must admit that I have been insulted. I have been vilified. While praying outside an abortion clinic, I was told, "Mr. Monk, go home to your comfortable life." I was going to say, "Come and join me for a day. You'll be walking on your knees by eleven o'clock at night." I decided it was prudent to denounce a photograph of a plastic crucifix immersed in the artist's urine, which was paid for by the National Endowment for the Arts. My fellow protesters and I were ridiculed for our criticism on the front page of a supposedly liberal Catholic weekly.

True Prudence

YES, LET'S BE REALLY PRUDENT. Let's have some common sense. Let's not expend our energy on useless activities. Let's not offend anyone unnecessarily. Let's get everything perfectly organized toward our eternal goal. I do not suggest that anyone be imprudent. I encourage everyone to be truly prudent, to seek first the kingdom of God and his justice, and all these things shall be added unto you. I ask you not to be afraid. Our Lord said to the apostles:

> Behold, I send you out as sheep in the midst of wolves; so be wise as serpents and innocent as doves. Beware of men; for they will deliver you up to councils, and flog you in their synagogues, and you will be dragged before governors and kings for my sake, to bear testimony before them and the Gentiles. When they deliver you up, do not be anxious how you are to speak or what you are to say; for what you are to say will be given to you in that hour; for it is not you who speak,

but the Spirit of your Father speaking through you. (Matthew 10:16–20)

Where were the humanly prudent apostles on Good Friday? Where were the imprudent women? The imprudent women were weeping along the Via Dolorosa. They also stood at the foot of the Cross, and they went to the tomb. Did you ever notice in the Stations of the Cross that the women come out way ahead of the men? The women are really the prudent ones, with a prudence of the spirit.

Pilate was trying to be prudent. He prudently avoided a riot and became the only canonized sinner in the history of the world. His name is mentioned at every Sunday Mass and in every Rosary as the one who killed Christ.

There is a photograph at the Dachau museum of SS officers at Buchenwald having a party. They're holding steins of beer, and a big German shepherd is sitting among them. They all look so happy, but they were on the wrong side. In six languages under the photograph it says, "And where are they now? Where are they now?"

A Christian Vision

THE REASON I MENTION personal things is that I have often been accused of imprudence by very nice people. My commitment to earthly imprudence began this way. I remember walking home one Christmas Eve from where I used to work for the Sisters of Saint Dominic, in the little town where I lived, Caldwell, New Jersey. And I said to myself, "If Jesus Christ had been born in Caldwell, where would He have been born?" There was a small black area with a little storefront church on Francisco Street. And I said, "If Jesus Christ were to be born in this town, He'd be born on that street." I was more and more convinced when I walked down the street and saw the modest homes and the place where African American people had to live. These were the times of "polite segregation" in the North.

I was barely a teenager in the mid-1940s. I decided then and there that I would do what I could to witness against racism. I did not know the word, but I could see that African American people were being misused. Many people did not understand my convictions that segregation was a sin against God and terribly hurtful to human beings. Its effects go back to the days of slavery and are still with us in the hopelessness, self-hatred, and lack of self-respect leading to crime, which has its source in anger and resentment and derails the lives of many young African Americans.

Prudence and Foolishness

ALL THESE THOUGHTS on different kinds of behavior may be confusing. Let me simply outline that there is prudence and there is foolishness. Within prudence there is supernatural prudence related to God's will and natural prudence related to the things we need in life. There is also false prudence, like those who go along with evil because they do not know what to do or because they are afraid of the consequences of opposition to the prevailing point of view.

How does a good Christian navigate through these muddy waters? The first step is to resolve to be prudent by following the Gospel teachings and the example of Christ. Second, the Christian must clearly distinguish between natural prudence, which seeks natural goodness, and supernatural goodness, which seeks the kingdom of God. They often fit together nicely, but sometimes they do not. Supernatural prudence may require a certain degree of discomfort or even risk of the things we cherish. Third, when we decide that we must remain silent out of prudence, because we cannot do anything in the face of a great evil, we must at least recall that our silence is not the best response. It is not wise according to the kingdom of God. It may be excusable, and it may be the only thing we can do at a given time, but it is a position we should try to avoid, if possible. Because of guilt about being foolishly prudent in the face of evil, we come to defend our imprudence as a virtue. This gets us trapped.

There is nothing wiser than to follow Christ. There is no surer way of happiness in this world than following the Gospel. The person who has sacrificed much in order to follow the supernatural goals set by our Lord Jesus Christ may look unfortunate in the eyes of the world, but he or she will have great interior peace. That alone makes supernatural prudence the wisest and most acceptable way to walk in this confusing world.

Please be prudent. These are dangerous times. Don't make any unnecessary enemies. Keep your eye on your goal, which is not the earthly goal of human acceptance, prosperity, comfort, or ambition. Be prudent. Seek first the kingdom of God and His justice, and all these things will be added unto you. "Every one who acknowledges me before men, I also will acknowledge before my Father who is in heaven; but whoever denies me before men, I also will deny before my Father who is in heaven" (Matthew 10:32–33).

And Saint Stephen said, "Behold, I see the heavens opened, and the Son of man standing at the right hand of God" (Acts 7:56). And he was killed for being supernaturally prudent. Be prudent. Be smart. Don't be stupid. But have the right kind of prudence.

Questions for Meditation on Prudence

1. What is the difference between natural and supernatural prudence?
2. How do the examples set forth in this chapter illustrate how the *Catechism of the Catholic Church* defines the virtue of prudence? (See the beginning of the chapter for the *Catechism* quote.)
3. How can you practice the virtue of prudence, as defined by the *Catechism* and illustrated in this chapter, in your daily life?
4. How did Our Lord exercise the virtue of prudence in His life?

Prayer

O Lord Jesus Christ, in every step of Your life You were guided by the Holy Spirit and by truth, which filled Your human and divine soul. I ask You to send Your Holy Spirit on me that I may judge things wisely in this world. It would be helpful if I had natural prudence, and I appreciate this gift. Most of all I want to have the prudence that You give, the prudence that seeks first the kingdom of God and His righteousness, and knows that all other things necessary will be given to me.

Help me to give an example of true prudence seeking the kingdom of God in all that I do, and help me avoid the false wisdom of the world and of things that pass away. Amen.

CHAPTER 2

Justice

When justice is done, it is a joy to the righteous, but dismay to evil-doers.

— PROVERBS 21:15

Justice *is the moral virtue that consists in the constant and firm will to give their due to God and neighbor. Justice toward God is called the "virtue of religion." Justice toward men disposes one to respect the rights of each and to establish in human relationships the harmony that promotes equity with regard to persons and to the common good. The just man, often mentioned in the Sacred Scriptures, is distinguished by habitual right thinking and the uprightness of his conduct toward his neighbor.*

— CATECHISM OF THE CATHOLIC CHURCH (N. 1807)

A S WITH PRUDENCE we distinguished between the natural and the supernatural virtues, so we will follow the same procedure with justice. The natural virtue of justice calls us to be fair and honest in our relationships with others, including God Himself. For this reason we will also consider in this chapter the natural virtue of religion, which directs us to honor God and observe the natural law and the norms of good behavior, which require all human beings to show reverence and gratitude to their Maker. The Christian virtue of justice makes us responsible for following the teachings of Christ and His Church with regard to all aspects of life. There is some overlapping of responsibilities between a Christian practice of justice to God and faith.

Justice is respected and demanded by almost everyone in the world. Almost all people have a sense of justice, even the very unjust. A psychological study was once done of people in prison, in which psychopaths — dangerous criminals who have no conscience — were compared with ordinary prisoners, those who may have been one-time offenders. Each group was asked to solve cases in ethics and morals, similar to those that might be given to seminarians to prepare them to hear confessions. The psychopaths did better than the ordinary prisoners. Psychopaths apparently have a sense of what's right and wrong, and they can apply it to others but not to themselves. If you have ever dealt with psychopaths, you realize that they might quickly say things like, "You call yourself a good Christian and that's what you're going to do to me." They can recognize that others act unjustly but not themselves. Psychopaths are blind in one eye — the eye that looks at themselves.

Justice and the Law

IN PUBLIC LIFE, there is often much talk about justice but little actual justice. This becomes obvious as the judicial system is more open to public scrutiny. How much is determined by the skill of lawyers? Sometimes the rich, who can afford highly skilled lawyers, literally get away with murder, whereas the poor often go to jail on little or no evidence. Don't ever get the idea that much of what is done in public life is an attempt to arrive at true justice. In fact, we get what we fight for, and the scales of justice are often tipped in favor of the wealthy and powerful.

I know a responsible young man who went to jail for several years. He claimed he was innocent, that the police planted narcotics on him. Later a dozen police officers in that precinct were indicted for criminal activities, including planting evidence on defendants, but that had no effect on the district attorney. Often officials are not out for justice. They want to get someone convicted or get someone off without any idea of justice.

Despite this, older courthouses of the United States almost always display a statue of Justice, an allegorical female figure with eyes blindfolded and holding scales in her hand. She symbolizes equal justice for all, but even in the best of circumstances justice is not always obtained. The same behavior in one town might get you a twenty-five-dollar fine and in the next town put you in jail for thirty days.

Do we always know what is just?

Yet everybody admires justice. It is a natural virtue and causes us to give everyone what is properly due them. But do we always know what is just? Who knows what is just when it comes to taxes or the family will? American affluence is sometimes the result of the exploitation and poverty of other, weaker countries. We are rich because someone else is poor.

Our foreign policy is often determined not by justice but by what is good for the American taxpayer. You may have investments in large corporations, which may do outrageously unjust things.

For example, when I was in the Philippines years ago giving a retreat, I came across a tribe of about eighty aboriginal people. From time immemorial they had owned a small mountain, where they lived and grazed their cattle. It was their whole world. It was theirs long before the Spaniards came to the Philippines, and no one had ever questioned their ownership. A Philippine corporation, said to be part of the Rockefeller empire, was taking the aborigines to court and confiscating their property, and they were defenseless because they had no deed. This was during the time of Ferdinand Marcos. The missionaries told me there was no way to save their mountain. Marcos had sold them out to a company owned ultimately by very rich Americans. Ownership of this little mountain, which had some natural resources, would go to the vast Rockefeller fortune, and a slice of that would go to support abortion throughout the world because that is an important cause of the Rockefeller Foundation.

Injustice in Our Backyard

WE LIKE TO THINK that one of our American ideals is justice. Yet one tenth of the initial capital of the United States — the foundational money of our country — was earned by slaves, the wages of a terrible injustice.

The cost of bananas remains relatively low because those who pick them work for very little. Don't stop buying bananas, because the harvesters need work, but realize that you may be participating in an injustice when you eat them. Do not think you can live in this world and not participate in injustice. Go on vacation to the Caribbean or Mexico, and you may be waited on by a smiling waiter in a white linen coat. His house, however, may have a dirt floor. The only plumbing may be a ditch in the backyard. Don't stop going on vacation, but realize that there is something terribly unequal about all of this. The earth's resources were given to the whole human race, and they are by no means equitably distributed. Some people work very hard for small wages. Others hardly work at all for immense amounts of money. Frequently, it is not skill but chance that determines that, or perhaps a kind of ruthlessness in human behavior.

People are often victims of incredible injustices. Years ago in the Pennsylvania coal region, immense areas were scarred, ripped-up for strip-mining. Many of these places were once owned by farmers. They had deeds to their property, but the deeds specified that they did not own the underground coal; therefore the coal companies could come and destroy their farms with no compensation. It is important to know that you cannot live in this very wealthy nation and not participate in some injustice.

This is why some people have said that charity and kindness to the poor are not just charity but also justice. We owe it. Some wealthy people recognize that. They regard themselves as stewards of what they have received. They are generous, but many others are not.

Justice is a strange thing. The pagans said, "The mills of the gods grind slowly, for they grind exceeding fine." The poor are not more unhappy than others. They are often desperately ill, they often have terrible calamities in their families, but from day to day they can laugh. It sometimes seems incredible, but they can enjoy life. This is a kind of divine justice. For example, the brothers of our community hold a block party every summer in our neighborhood. It's one of the poorer streets in the city. Some of the children have lost one or both of their parents to AIDS. They're cared for by an aunt or a grandmother. However, they have a marvelous time at the block party. The big entertainment is filling balloons with water and throwing them at one another. The food is plain, but they enjoy themselves because they don't have anything else. Happiness is an extremely subjective phenomenon.

When I was in high school, I used to caddy at an expensive country club. I never realized until later that all the caddies were white. The only African Americans were those who washed dishes. I thought many wealthy club members were unhappy. They certainly didn't look happy, and some were terribly impolite. My father was a construction engineer who carried a lunch box to work. We had a large family. We did not belong to a country club, but we had good manners. Some members of the club were so impolite that I used to wonder, "Didn't their mothers ever teach them anything?" It was while working at the club that I decided that my inspiration to become a friar was valid, and I said good-bye to the whole place.

> **On Judgment Day, we will be asked what we did with the things that we received. How did we observe the virtue of justice? How shall we answer?**

Members of the Church too often participate in injustice. Representatives of the Church can be just as oblivious as other people of their responsibilities concerning justice. Parish and diocesan workers often do not receive an adequate wage. In recent years, Catholic institutions, paid for by the hard work of the faithful, have been simply given up, surrendered, and abandoned. This is true of many Catholic colleges, which were once an integral part of our responsibility to evangelize, but which now have become completely secularized. It is important to keep in mind that the change from thriving Catholic colleges to completely secular institutions was not the result of some hostile government takeover, or the suppression of religious institutions by revolutionary forces inimical to the faith. The change was initiated, orchestrated, and approved by the Catholic religious communities that had founded the schools. Those whose money built the colleges gave that money for Catholic education. What has become of the sacrificial giving of earlier generations? Justice, even on a natural level, has hardly been observed. At the final judgment, such questions will be asked.

This brings up the question of what will happen to the institutions Catholics support today with their money. Will they too be betrayed? It is strange how we take injustice in stride. The Church bureaucracies can be very unjust, and their members can commit as many injustices as anyone else. Catholics have no monopoly on any virtue, and it is time we realized it. Consequently, we must struggle every day to be just. On Judgment Day, we will be asked what we did with the things that we received. How did we observe the virtue of justice? How shall we answer?

What to Do About Injustice

IF YOU FEEL GUILTY about some of this injustice, then generosity is a great way out, especially if you're not looking for too much thanks. We could begin with generosity with those who work in restaurants, taxi drivers, and others who work for tips. We can make a habit of showing generosity toward those who work at menial jobs and who are often not treated well. And we can support laws that give a better chance to those who are victims of injustice.

The Justice of God

IT DOESN'T MAKE MUCH sense to say that God is prudent. But God is just. He does not *do* justice; He *is* justice. He is also mercy, beauty, and truth. But He is not capable of injustice. In the economy of salvation, which we do not understand, justice required, in some mysterious ways, the holy life and terrible death of Jesus Christ. That death was not required by God, but was required apparently by divine Justice. Christ had to come into the world and be subject to the same vicissitudes of life as the rest of us, the same vulnerability to outrageous injustice. He would call the world to the kingdom of God, but it would not listen. Be clear in your mind that God did not will Christ's crucifixion. God willed Christ's Incarnation. Christ's crucifixion was the result of Judas Iscariot, the high priests, Pontius Pilate, Herod, and many others. Christ called the world to salvation. He did not have to die to redeem the world. His becoming human justified us all. Theologians say that we were adopted as children of God by the Incarnation. It is true that the prophecies of the Old Testament foretold the death of the Messiah, but the prophecies were given because God knew what was going to happen to His Son as a consequence of people's free will.

Prophecies do not make things happen. It is, rather, the other way round: Things that are going to happen make prophecies occur. This is a mystery. If you wonder whether God is just, consider the life, passion, and death of Jesus Christ. In some way the books had to be balanced. The evil had to be undone. As it says in the epistle to the Hebrews, the price had to be paid. It did not have to be that terrible a price, but it became so terrible because of the ill will of human beings.

People tell me, "I think everybody's going to heaven." Is that so? What about the parables of Jesus Christ? Was He lying when He gave us the parables? The parables are the very voice of Christ, and almost all of the parables speak of the Last Judgment, and many of them warn us about eternal loss. If you have trouble believing in hell, go to the Holocaust museum in Washington or visit Auschwitz. Then you will believe in hell. You will take the words of Christ very seriously.

The Christian's Obligation to Justice

CHRISTIAN JUSTICE CAUSES us to give to God what is due Him and, within that understanding, to give to others what is due them as children of God. Christians have a much greater responsibility to justice. We must be more aware of the fact that we all accidentally participate in injustice, that we are well-off because others are poor, and that without ever willing it, we reap the fruits of economic exploitation and impoverishment.

Private property is by no means an absolute right. It is limited by justice, and it is, to some degree, a fiction of law. Who owns the world? God owns the world. We are lent little pieces of it, and no ownership is absolute. It is all contingent on justice. We hope that the civil law at times reflects that justice, but whether it does or not, the divine law is there because God Himself is justice.

Religion and Faith

GOD HAS CERTAIN NATURAL rights by the natural virtue of justice. All worship of God is not the same as the virtue of faith. Worship involves the virtue of religion, which is part of the virtue of justice. In *The Book of Virtues*, William Bennett mentions faith, which, he points out, is a supernatural virtue. He writes:

> Faith, hope, and love are formally regarded as theological virtues in traditional Christian doctrine. They

mark dispositions in persons who are flourishing in life from that religious perspective.

There are theological virtues, and they flow from grace. He says, however, there is nothing distinctively Christian in recognizing that religious faith adds a significant dimension to moral life worldwide. Religious faith is the source of discipline and power and meaning in the lives of the faithful of any major religious creed. It is a force made powerful by human experience; a shared faith binds people together in ways that cannot be duplicated by any other means.

What Bennett is really talking about is a subdivision of the virtue of justice called the *virtue of religion*, for which most feel a need. Something like 92 or 94 percent of Americans polled have said that they not only pray but they also believe that Someone hears their prayer. That is not necessarily faith. It might simply be the operation of the virtue of religion. Many people think they have faith, but what they really have is natural religion, a part of justice. There is a worldly religiosity, and it exists even in Christianity. It is the natural foundation for the supernatural virtue of faith, but it is not to be mistaken for faith.

We sometimes meet people who are pillars of the Church but completely lacking in charity. At least they have faith, we say — but they probably do not. What they have is religiosity. They are often unkind and grasping or terribly judgmental. They see the Church or the parish as their own possession and social club. They may be out for prestige. They are unwelcoming to the poor and strangers. They may possess religiosity, but they are not Christians.

Some years ago, Children's Village, where I was once chaplain, opened a group home in the borough of Queens, in New

York City. It was not in a prosperous area, and we belonged to a parish on the edge of the neighborhood. A number of the boys in the group home were Hispanic or black, and I arranged for them all, Protestants and Catholics, to go to church on Sunday. The following week I asked the Catholics, "Did you go to Mass?"

"Yeah," they said, "but we ain't going back."

"Why not?"

"All we got was hard looks."

"Oh," I said. "We will go next Sunday, and I will go with you."

We went to the eleven o'clock Mass and sat in the front row. There were hard looks, but some of them came from me. If anyone had said anything to me, I would have told them that they were not Christians, but only religiously oriented people. How many times does the natural virtue of religion masquerade as Christian faith? Our Lord tells us, "Not every one who says to me, 'Lord, Lord,' shall enter the kingdom of heaven" (Matthew 7:21).

The Jewish religion, to which our Lord belonged, was both a supernatural faith founded by God on Abraham, Moses, and the prophets, and a folk religion of a people who at that moment were under Roman occupation. It was both a national identity and a religious faith. It was truly a faith because it was given by God. Saint Paul pointed out with his usual eloquence that some did better than others, although they all had the same experience of God:

> I want you to know, brethren, that our fathers were all under the cloud, and all passed through the sea, and all were baptized into Moses in the cloud and in the sea, and all ate the same supernatural food and all drank

the same supernatural drink. For they drank from the supernatural Rock which followed them, and the Rock was Christ. Nevertheless with most of them God was not pleased; for they were overthrown in the wilderness. (1 Corinthians 10:1–5)

In Northern Ireland, the violent conflict between Catholics and Protestants is not over faith. It is about national identity united to religion. It's about memories of injustices long ago and at the present time — economic and other injustices — but it is not a clash of faiths. It is religion that has ceased to be a virtue.

We should all practice the virtue of religion, on which faith is built. We should respect any good religion that makes people pray to God and behave themselves. That is what we have in common with Hindus and Buddhists. We do not have a faith in common with them, but we have a respect for the virtue of religion. The first thing that the virtue of religion does is to make us take God seriously. We see how terribly weak this virtue is in our culture. Can our culture be called reverent? Is there reverence for life? Look at the entertainment. What is on television every day? Killing people. Everybody wonders why some youngsters kill people. It's what they see all day on television.

When Roman civilization was in decline, the emperors provided bread and circuses. The circuses were combats in which gladiators killed one another and Christians were fed to the lions. Now the equivalent in violence can be seen on television. We condemn the Romans for their barbarism, but are we any better? Don't we have a constant diet of death and destruction for entertainment?

Reverence and Religion

WE HEAR PEOPLE SAY, "I don't go to church. I don't get anything out of it." We should get something out of it, but that is quite secondary. We go to church — to Mass — to worship and give reverence to God, to give thanks for sight, hearing, smell, taste, touch, life, time, and a host of other blessings. What is our attitude toward God? Is it one of reverence? Do we show reverence to His Presence in the Blessed Sacrament? We must examine ourselves often and deeply on these questions. How do we fall short?

Venerable John Henry Newman (1801–1890), one of the profoundly religious men of the nineteenth century, maintains that we will never come to a knowledge of God until we are reverent. Without reverence we do not even have the virtue of religion, which for the Christian should open the door to faith. In Catholic higher education, there has been widespread irreverence toward God and His teachings, especially in the name of Scripture studies. There is not a Catholic in the country who has not witnessed serious institutionalized liturgical abuse and irreverence.

Saint Augustine is very critical of bishops who "do not oversee the flock of Christ."[18] They are bishops in name only, who do not go before the flock, leading them and defending them from wolves. Our Lord, on the other hand, presents Himself to us as the Good Shepherd. The good bishop is to model himself on Christ and be ready to lay down his life for his people:

> He who is a hireling and not a shepherd, whose own the sheep are not, sees the wolf coming and leaves the sheep and flees; and the wolf snatches them and

scatters them. He flees because he is a hireling and cares nothing for the sheep. (John 10:12–13)

Cardinal Newman had a great sense of religion combined with a great Christian faith, and he was certainly one of the most brilliant men of his time. Because there is so much religious indifference in our day, I will use several citations from his sermons. They should strengthen the faith of believers and at the same time cast some light on the process by which people arrive at irreligion or the denial of faith.

It is an old strategy of people half interested in religion but unwilling to commit themselves to following Christ and His Gospel that they will listen but not hear. Our Lord's words apply to most of the religious intelligentsia and their students. They have ears but they do not hear, eyes but they do not see (see Matthew 13:13–17). Newman's observations sum up a great deal of "interest in religion" that never comes to faith:

For is not this the error, the common and fatal error, of the world, to think itself a judge of Religious Truth without preparation of heart? "I am the good Shepherd, and know My sheep, and am known of Mine." "He goeth before them, and the sheep follow Him, for they know His voice." "The pure in heart shall see God:" "to the meek mysteries are revealed;" "he that is spiritual judgeth all things." "The darkness comprehendeth it not." Gross eyes see not; heavy ears hear not. But in the schools of the world the ways towards Truth are considered high roads open to all men, however disposed, at all times. Truth is to be approached without homage. Every one is considered on a level with his neighbour; or rather the powers of the intellect, acuteness, sagacity, subtlety, and depth, are thought the guides into Truth. Men consider that they have as full a right to discuss religious subjects, as if they were themselves religious. They will enter upon the most sacred points of Faith at the moment, at their pleasure, — if it so happen, in a careless frame of mind, in their hours of recreation, over the wine cup. Is it wonderful that they so frequently end in becoming indifferentists, and conclude that Religious Truth is but a name, that all men are right and all wrong, from witnessing externally the multitude of sects and parties, and from the clear consciousness they possess within, that their own inquiries end in darkness?[19]

Everyone complains about the Church's bad old days before the Second Vatican Council, but in those days there was at least a sense of reverence. No one talked in Church. Alan Watts, who was an Episcopalian writer, lamented the fact that the last place in the Western world where great silence could be experienced in public — at the consecration of the Catholic Mass — had been lost.

The first thing we owe God is reverence and respect. Respect means that we recognize that He is infinite. No creature ever plumbs the depths of God's infinity. We don't even have a concept of infinity. Albert Einstein said that those who cannot look on the mysteries in the universe with wonder and awe might as well be dead. He called his religion a "humble admiration of the illimitable superior spirit who reveals himself in the slight details we are able to perceive with our frail and feeble minds."[20]

Religion and Faith

IF WE GO BEYOND justice and the religion we owe to God and look at faith (as we will do), we realize that the Christian responsibilities are much more demanding. According to the Catholic faith, Christ is the eternal Son of God, second Person of the Blessed Trinity, existing before all ages. He emptied Himself and took on a human nature and a human soul at a point in time, but the divine Person existed from all eternity and will always exist. The Person did not come to exist when the man began. He was an infinite, divine Person before that. It is therefore incredible irreverence to claim that our Lord Jesus Christ did not know who He was, as some skeptical "Christian" scholars do. When we speak of Christ or of the Scriptures, we must do so with profound reverence.

We owe God reverence, and we owe Him obedience. Questions about God's existence or attributes can be asked with sincerity, but they are often asked with irreverence. It is profoundly irreverent to say off-handedly, "Well, I don't think there is a God" or "Does it really matter if there is a God?"

People in former times, before the so-called Enlightenment, thought differently. They might at times have acted as though there were no God, but they would not have said that He did not exist. The real question is: Has God revealed Himself to His people? Quite apart from Scripture, reason certainly favors the supposition. Newman put it this way:

> Revelation, far from suspicious, is borne in upon our hearts by the strongest presumptions of reason in its behalf. It is hard to believe that it has not been given, as indeed the conduct of mankind has ever shown. You cannot help expecting it from the hands of the

All-merciful, unworthy as you feel yourselves of it. It is not that you can claim it, but that He inspires hope of it; it is not you that are worthy of the gift, but it is the gift which is worthy of your Creator. It is so urgently probable, that little evidence is required for it, even though but little were given.... The very fact that there is a Creator, and a hidden one, powerfully bears you on and sets you down at the very threshold of revelation, and leaves you there looking up earnestly for Divine tokens that a revelation has been made.[21]

Men are too well inclined to sit at home, instead of stirring themselves to inquire whether a revelation has been given; they expect its evidences to come to them without their trouble.[22]

The refusal by so many today to admit of God — either as a Being or as a presence in their lives — is an example of modern man's deep irreverence.

On the other hand, there is the religious mind:

A religious mind is ever marvelling, and irreligious men laugh and scoff at it because it marvels. A religious mind is ever looking out of itself, is ever pondering God's words, is ever "looking into" them with the Angels, is ever realizing to itself Him on whom it depends, and who is the centre of all truth and good. Carnal and proud minds are contented with self; they like to remain at home; when they hear of mysteries, they have no devout curiosity to go and see the great sight, though it be ever so little out of their way; and when it actually falls in their path, they stumble at it.

As great then as is the difference between hanging upon the thought of God and resting in ourselves, lifting up the heart to God and bringing all things in heaven and earth down to ourselves, exalting God and exalting reason, measuring things by God's power and measuring them by our own ignorance, so great is the difference between him who believes in the Christian mysteries and him who does not. And were there no other reason for the revelation of them, but this gracious one, of raising us, refining us, making us reverent, making us expectant and devout, surely this would be more than a sufficient one.[23]

While it is true that some people are too credulous, even superstitious, about private revelations, others with little thought will assume they could never happen.[24] They therefore dismiss shrines like Lourdes, Fátima, or Paray-le-Monial, and discount the revelations of God's love for the human race through the Sacred Heart of Jesus. The skeptics might accept Saint Francis because he spoke to the birds and wrote nice prayers, but they would forget that he also had visions of Christ and received the stigmata. They favor a Christ walking through the fields and greeting the lepers, but they are intimidated by the thought that He cured and that He rose physically from the dead. They lack any sense of mystery or wonder. They reduce religion to something they can measure with their own limited minds.

Many things in life go beyond the limitations of the human mind. Physical and moral cures at places like Lourdes cannot be accounted for by human reason any more than the miraculous image of Our Lady at the shrine in Guadalupe, in Mexico. It is not the product of painting, weaving, dying, or photography. How did it get there? It is a mystery. If you have never gone as a pilgrim to a great shrine, you have missed a powerful religious experience. You may have missed what might have been the high point in your life. When we discuss the virtue of faith, we will discuss much more about what goes beyond religion.

God's Justice and My Own

GOD IS JUST. He not only expects things of us but He also rewards those who fulfill their obligation. Those who believe in Him and are loyal to Him in the greatest difficulties will be rewarded. He does not fail. God is just — in this life and at the end of this life. When someone dies, there may be things in them that need to be resolved: sins to be forgiven, bad attitudes to be overcome, unforgivenesses to be transcended, deep resentments even against close family members. This is where we get the beautiful concept of purgatory. I always thought purgatory was the most obvious thing in the world. Because of God's justice and holiness, we must be cleansed of our remaining faults and imperfections

> Are you just? To those you meet? To family, friends, enemies? Are you just to the memory of those who are dead?

before we can enter the presence of the all-holy God. Christ paid the price for our salvation by His terrible death on the Cross, but we must cooperate with the grace of salvation and accept it all the way. Our purgation begins in this life, but depending on our degree of cooperation, it may have to be finished in the next.

Are you just? To those you meet? To family, friends, enemies? Are you just to the memory of those who are dead? Do you owe your parents something that you didn't thank them for enough? Are you indebted to surrogate parents — teachers and others who befriended you in childhood? Do you owe something to close relatives, a spouse, brothers or sisters? Are there unpaid debts?

God is just. They will have to be paid. Jesus tells us that they are paid to the last penny (see Matthew 5:26). He has done His best to pay them for us, but we must do our part.

Do we use too much of this world's goods? Do we use them improperly? Do we think of the poor? Sometimes others are poor because we are well-off. Do we speak to people about justice? We can be certain that when we die, every bit of injustice in our soul will be resolved. Have we been just toward God, to those we know and love, and to the poor and the needy? Think of the incredible injustice done to unborn children and to poor unwed mothers forced into abortion.

We live in an age of great injustice. Justice is talked about much but little practiced. It is a bitter experience to help someone obtain justice and then watch as they are unjust to others. Who is to say that the victim will be just when he is no longer a victim? It is not important to me what a person does with the justice that I give him. Dorothy Day used to say that what we give to the poor is owed to them in justice; it is not charity. When we see the homeless in the street, they may not ask for anything, but it would be a work of justice to give them something. They may be mentally ill and abandoned by the state, whose responsibility it is, in justice, to care for them.

Is the taking of an innocent person's life just? Even religious bodies can be unjust. That is why they have judicial procedures in order to correct their own injustice. On Judgment Day, the injustice we have suffered in this world will be taken away, but we will be asked if we have worked for justice. How blessed are they who hunger and thirst for justice, for they shall be filled — because God is not simply just. God *is* justice. He is also mercy and love. One attribute of the Divine Being cannot exist without the others. Thank God He is merciful and forgiving, because if we were operating on pure justice, we would all be lost. We also must be just and make up for our injustice by helping those harmed by sins that, according to the Bible, cry to heaven for vengeance. Such sins include depriving the poor of their just wages and defrauding the widow and the orphan.

Justice sometimes requires that we speak out. It always requires that we be reverent to God and His works. If I were granted one wish, it would be that all Christians and other believers be reverent before God. If they were, all these other things would fall into place. Our Lord says, "Seek first his kingdom and his righteousness, and all these things shall be yours as well" (Matthew 6:33).

And the preparation for justice is reverence to God.

Questions for Meditation on Justice

1. How is the *Catechism*'s definition of justice (see quote at the beginning of this chapter) illustrated in this chapter?
2. What is the justice that we "owe" God?
3. What is the justice that we "owe" our neighbor? Who is our neighbor? (Read Luke 10:29–37.)
4. How can you concretely practice the virtue of justice in your daily life?

Prayer

O Lord Jesus Christ, You lived in a world filled with injustice, and You were the victim of the most frightful injustice ever committed. Yet, You called people to be just and merciful. You always taught Your disciples to put their duties to God first, but You never failed to recognize their duties to men. Often You did not make sharp distinctions between charity and justice, seeking always to give as much as You could from Your divine love. Thus, in Your holy life, justice and love are not greatly distinguished. In our lives, we must first seek to be just and then to be loving. Help us, O Lord, by Your Holy Spirit, to follow in Your righteous way, the way of charity and justice, always placing first Your strongest and most powerful teaching that we must love both justly and generously. Amen.

CHAPTER 3

Fortitude

Be strong, and let your heart take courage, all you who wait for the
LORD!

— PSALM 31:24

Fortitude *is the moral virtue that ensures firmness in difficulties and*
constancy in the pursuit of the good. It strengthens the resolve to
resist temptations and to overcome obstacles in the moral life. The
virtue of fortitude enables one to conquer fear, even fear of death, and
to face trials and persecutions. It disposes one even to renounce and
sacrifice his life in defense of a just cause. "The Lord is my strength
and my song" (Psalm 118:14). "In the world you have tribulation;
but be of good cheer, I have overcome the world" (John 16:33).

— CATECHISM OF THE CATHOLIC CHURCH (N. 1808)

ON A VISIT TO ROME some years ago, a group of American bishops were greeted by Pope John Paul II with one
word: *Coraggio* ("courage"). We live in an age that requires
much courage. No sooner did the Church see the collapse and
fall of one of its greatest enemies in modern times — Marxist
communism — than it was surrounded by enemies on all sides.

In addition, there are the Judases within, who, like the darnel in the Gospel parable, have always existed in the Church's field of wheat, but whose betrayal of Christ and His Church has been particularly obvious in the decades after Vatican II.

Pope John Paul II was a seminarian in Poland during the days of Nazi occupation. Had he been found out, it would have meant death or transferal to a slave labor camp. Throughout his life he remained an example of courage. *Courage* means strength or fortitude in danger, but also in the daily round and challenges of life. It might take more courage just to get up on certain days than it would to face a great danger. Difficulties, setbacks, misunderstandings, failures, deep hurts — all of these require *coraggio*.

This moral virtue is recognized and admired by all people. Every nation that has grown, developed, and made its mark on history has had its heroes and stories of courage. One of the signs of a society in decline, like our own, is the absence of admiration for people of courage. Our country was founded by men who said in effect, "Either we hang together or we will hang alone." Signers of the Declaration of Independence were *ipso facto* traitors to the British crown, to which they owed allegiance. Had they been arrested, they would have been liable to death.

Many of us are descended from people who courageously faced the long sea voyage to America and the dangers in beginning over in what was often a hostile environment. Most of us are children of the Catholic immigration, those Europeans who came to the United States in the nineteenth and early twentieth centuries, passing through the immigration centers at Ellis Island and Castle Garden in New York. It took courage to face the unknown, and either a better life or certain death in an alien land. When they arrived, they had to be examined, and they would do all sorts of things so that they didn't cough or look sick, in order to get through the medical inspection and be registered.

Most of the slums of New York are dotted with huge churches, synagogues, and schools built by immigrants, and large cemeteries where they are buried. They built an immense structure of religious and social institutions that took care of them and their children from cradle to grave, and they did it on a few pennies an hour. How? With courage.

Sadly, we don't admire courage much anymore in our country. There is no message of courage. The Vietnam War memorial in Washington shows three soldiers with terror written on their faces. Older war memorials show courage. It is a natural virtue that makes people willing to face extreme danger or to endure great difficulty over a period of time in order to accomplish a decent goal they have set for themselves. It is to be distinguished from bravado, or foolhardiness, which characterizes a selfish, egotistical goal.

Christian Courage

THE SUPERNATURAL CHRISTIAN virtue of courage enables someone to face danger and endure great difficulty to achieve the ultimate goal of salvation or help others achieve the same goal. Keep in mind that natural virtues have as their goal a good, decent life in this world; the same qualities touched by the grace of the Holy Spirit have for their goal eternal life. One doesn't cancel out the other. We can have both natural and supernatural courage; we can also have one and not the other.

In addition to being a virtue (natural and supernatural), courage is so important that it is also one of the gifts of the Holy Spirit. The seven gifts of the Holy Spirit are quite different from virtues. In some respects, they are almost the opposite. The gifts of the Holy Spirit are given to people who sometimes do not have a particular personal quality but who receive it by God's grace. So the gifts of the Holy Spirit could make a brave person out of a coward, or a good counselor out of a fool.

The notion of courage as an ideal is certainly reduced in our society because of selfism. If I am an important person in a worldly sense and my biggest intent in life is obtaining plea-sure and achieving my potential, I will not be interested in courage. I won't want to lose my life for someone else. I won't want to carry the ball for Harvard or lead the Light Brigade. Nor do I value endurance. The corollary to seeking pleasure, of course, is avoiding discomfort in any form. Are you slightly uncomfort-able during the summer heat? Get an air conditioner as quick-ly as possible. Have you got a headache? Stuff yourself with aspirins or Tylenol. Is your throat a little scratchy? Run — do not walk — to the nearest pharmacy and buy every cold rem-edy on the shelf. Medicate yourself into a stupor and then col-lar everyone who comes along (if no one comes along, phone everyone you know) and let them know how much you are suf-fering. Ah, selfism!

> The notion of courage as an ideal is certainly reduced in our society because of selfism.

But how does any of this square with Christianity? Our religion was founded by the One who said, "If any man would come after me, let him deny himself and take up his cross and follow me. For whoever would save his life will lose it, and whoever loses his life for my sake will find it" (Matthew 16:24–25). And again, "They will put you out of the syna-gogues; indeed, the hour is coming when whoever kills you will think he is offering service to God" (John 16:2). These are not exactly cheerful tidings. We deny the dark side of Christianity. Crucifixes that once reminded us of Christ's sacrifice for the salvation of the world have been replaced in church by not terribly convincing statues of the Resurrection. We have attempted to block out the challenge of Christianity: the Cross.

Many years ago, Cardinal Terence Cooke had the idea of starting an organization for Catholic homosexuals to help them lead a chaste life. The organization is called Courage, because that's what it takes — a lot of courage. It calls people to a challenge, including some members of the clergy. An interesting detail is that the name Courage was chosen by the first members as a contrast to the name of another group that does not encourage chastity — namely, Dignity, which is obviously a more self-centered concept.

Unfortunately, the trend today is to make everything easy, to take away the challenges of life. This defeats the most important aspect of courage, which is patient endurance and willingness to continue over the long haul in difficult situations.

One of the bravest people I ever met was Father Walter Ciszek, S.J., who was officially dead and came back to life. He was ordained a Jesuit in Rome, and his one goal was to work in Russia. He managed to get there in 1939, after which nobody heard anymore about him. In 1943 or 1944, the Jesuits announced his death and had a funeral Mass said for the repose of his soul. About twenty years later, he came back from the dead. He had been in Siberia, where he gave thirty-day retreats in the concentration camps. He wrote two fascinating books about his experiences, *With God in Russia* and *He Leadeth Me*.

Another courageous person was Monsignor Arthur Rojek, who spent four and a half years in Auschwitz, Buchenwald, and Dachau. When he was released by the Americans, he weighed sixty-five pounds, and he was a man six feet three and at the edge of death. I asked him, "What did you think the day you came out?" He said, "I thought, 'I can handle anything life can give me now.'"

It is a virtuous thing to suffer with those who suffer and to mourn with those who mourn. Our Lord says, "Blessed are those who mourn" (Matthew 5:4). On the other hand, He also calls us to pick up our cross and carry it. I do not say we shouldn't mourn, but we should keep busy while we mourn. When the mourning is over, we should already be back to work. It is very difficult for the more affluent segment of society to do this. The poor have got to go back to work. The affluent can afford to stay home and be miserable.

People who picket abortion clinics risk arrest, jail time, and stiff fines. It takes courage. Our society does not encourage people to be courageous. It thinks that those who hold opposing views are crazy. For this reason even Christians have a very conservative attitude toward protesting. The merely pious, as distinct from the really devout, think that public protest is a bit over the top. It is worth meditating on this and asking ourselves with our present attitudes whether we would have been willing to follow the itinerant preacher who had seriously annoyed the powers that be.

> It is worth meditating on this and asking ourselves with our present attitudes whether we would have been willing to follow the itinerant preacher who had seriously annoyed the powers that be.

Christian Courage and Daily Life

MANY PEOPLE SAY to me, "I'm so discouraged. I raised four kids, sent them all to Catholic schools, and none of them go to church." That's a very big hurt, but don't sit around weeping and lamenting. Give them a copy of the *Catechism* for Christmas. Be a pest. Invite them to go to church. When they tell you they lost their job, ask them when they last said a prayer. Let them know that you are not angry, only hurt and disappointed.

Many people have to put up with difficult spouses. Somehow in the United States we have got the idea that everybody has to be happy, that every marriage will be ideal. Saint Augustine, who was a great realist, spoke about virtues:

> When virtues are genuine virtues — and that is possible only when men believe in God — they make no pretense of protecting their possessors from unhappiness, for that would be a false promise; but they do claim that human life, now compelled to feel the misery of so many grievous ills on earth, can, by the hope of heaven, be made both happy and secure.[25]

We say that hope in the face of difficulty makes courage possible. It is not the hope that everything will be easy or happy; it is hope in eternal life.

Augustine continues:

> Remember the troubles of lovers listed by . . . Terence:
>
> > Slights and fights and spirits vexed,
> > War today and peace the next.
>
> All human relationships are fraught with such misunderstandings. Not even the pure-hearted affection of friends is free from them. All history is a tale of "slights and fights and spirits vexed," and we must expect such unpleasantness as an assured thing, whereas peace is a

good unguaranteed — dependent upon the unknowable interior dispositions of our friends. Even if we could read their hearts today, anything might happen tomorrow. Take the members of a single family. Who are as fond of one another as, in general, they are or, at least, are expected to be? Yet who can rely utterly even on family affection? How much unhappiness has sprung from the ambush of domestic disloyalties! And how galling the disillusionment after peace had been so sweet, or seemed to be, though in fact it was nothing but a clever counterfeit. That is why no one can read without a sigh those touching words of Cicero: "No snares are ever so insidious as those lurking as dutiful devotion or labeled as family affection. You can easily escape from an open foe, but when hatred lurks in the bosom of a family, it has taken a position and pounced upon you before it can be spied out or recognized for what it is."

Even divine revelation reminds us: "And a man's enemies will be those of his own household" (Matthew 10:36). It breaks the heart of any good man to hear this, for even if he be brave enough to bear, or vigilant enough to beware of, the ruses of faithless friends, he must suffer greatly just the same when he discovers how treacherous they are. And it makes no difference whether they were genuine friends who have turned traitors, or traitorous men who had been trading on pretended affection all along.[26]

We must continue through life with courage; as Christians, we must even go on with forgiveness and love. The heart of family life is not only affection but also forgiveness. It is not having good times together, but carrying each other's cross. Many remain faithful and true in the most difficult of circumstances; they do not run from the battle. What sustains them is Christian hope. We can muddle through this world and hope that things will get better, which is natural courage. Our hope, however, should be for the other side. Courage comes from grace and is founded on Christ's promise of eternal life with Him.

A woman once phoned me to say that after a long time she had finally gotten good news. Her daughter, who for ten years had been a drug addict, had finally been arrested. At last there was some hope, because she could be referred by the court for some kind of help. This woman was both a realist and a believer. We must go on with hope in God's mercy and hope beyond this world. Courage and hope go together.

What about the timid, men or women who are fearful? There is work for the Holy Spirit to do.

Monsignor Rojek told me that when Americans liberated Dachau, their tanks knocked down the gate. Over it, previously hidden by the lintel, was one word: *Spes*, the Latin word for hope. It probably had been surreptitiously placed there by a prisoner who was a priest. Out of every ten who died at Dachau, one was a Catholic priest.

What about the timid, men or women who are fearful? There is work for the Holy Spirit to do. The following story will help to put it in some perspective.

In the opera *Dialogues of the Carmelites*, which is set during the French Revolution, one of the characters, Blanche de la Force, leaves the monastery where she is a novice, when faced with almost certain death at the guillotine.[27] The rest of the community, who have made a promise to undergo martyrdom, are imprisoned and sentenced to death. The point here, of course, is that the community symbolizes faith and fortitude, while Blanche represents timidity. On the day of the execution, however, as the nuns make their way up the scaffold singing *Veni, Sancte Spiritus*, they are joined by Blanche, who, fortified now by Holy Spirit with the gift of courage, is prepared to make the heroic sacrifice of her life, and the opera ends on a note of tragedy and triumph. Obviously, the members of the community were able to give their lives in that manner as a result of the virtue and gift of courage. Blanche's martyrdom, on the other hand, was solely the result of the gift of the Holy Spirit.

Those who are open to receiving the gifts of the Holy Spirit will have more courage than they ever had. Brave people doing courageous things are not nearly as impressive as the timid acting with courage. With the latter we see the pure work of God. All through the Church's history, the most unlikely people have been called to martyrdom. Quite ordinary people — housewives, little girls, and cobblers — and aristocrats have made the ultimate sacrifice to witness to Christ and the truth of His Church, often enduring slow, agonizing deaths. But under an unremarkable exterior they have been tough. Saint Lawrence the deacon, for example, was roasted alive on a kind of grill, quipping to his tormentors, "Turn me over. I'm done on this side." Many of the English martyrs met their deaths not only with unflinching courage but also with great humor. As he reached the place of his execution, Saint Thomas More said, "I pray thee, Master Lieutenant, see me safe up. As for my coming down, I'll shift for myself." Saint John Fisher handed his cane to the axe man and said, "I won't be needing this anymore."

I once said Mass at the tomb of Father Miguel Pro, the Mexican Jesuit martyr during the persecution of the Church in the 1920s. He continued to work as a priest, even baptizing children publicly near the presidential residence, until he was arrested and executed before a firing squad. There are photos of him, with arms outstretched, rosary in his hand. His last words were, "Long live Christ the King!"

Sometimes it is much harder to look every day at disappointment, dashed hopes, betrayal, failures, and hopelessness than it is to look down the barrel of a gun. Sometimes the greatest test of courage is in the face of terminal illness. If we ask for the gift of courage, we will receive it. Most people are afraid to ask, which is why they don't receive it. When we consider the deaths of courageous people, known and unknown, past and present, it should spur us on to ask for the grace of courage, the greatest gift even at the end.

Questions for Meditation on Fortitude

1. How do the stories in this chapter illustrate the *Catechism*'s definition of fortitude found at the beginning of the chapter?
2. In what ways do you exercise this virtue in your life? Where might you be more courageous in following Christ?
3. How can facing difficulties with fortitude help you?
4. If you are timid by nature, what might you do to live out this virtue?

Prayer

Lord Jesus Christ, in all Your life there were fearful things, and You overcame all obstacles or faced them to the bitter end, when there was no way out. However, You give us incredible examples of the battle to be courageous in the human mind. In Your agony in the garden, You show us that even in Your humanity You experienced fear and a battle between escape and acceptance of the bitter reality that was to come. You give us this wonderful example so that when there is fear in our lives, we know that we can overcome it with Your grace.

O merciful Savior, goodness and love for souls brought You to a terrible suffering and death. When we face the difficulties and darkness of life, including our own passion, give us the grace to follow Your example in Gethsemane. Help us to say to the heavenly Father, "Your will be done." Amen.

CHAPTER 4

Temperance

◦━━━━◦

For the grace of God has appeared for the salvation of all men, train-ing us to renounce irreligion and worldly passions, and to live sober, upright, and godly lives in this world, awaiting our blessed hope, the appearing of the glory of our great God and Savior Jesus Christ, who gave himself for us to redeem us from all iniquity and to purify for himself a people of his own who are zealous for good deeds.

— TITUS 2:11–14

Temperance *is the moral virtue that moderates the attraction of pleasures and provides balance in the use of created goods. It ensures the will's mastery over instincts and keeps desires within the limits of what is honorable. The temperate person directs the sensitive appetites toward what is good and maintains a healthy discretion: "Do not follow your inclination and strength, walking according to the desires of your heart" (Sirach 5:2). Temperance is often praised in the Old Testament: "Do not follow your base desires, but restrain your appetites" (Sirach 18:30).*

— CATECHISM OF THE CATHOLIC CHURCH (N. 1809)

TEMPERANCE AS A VIRTUE has had a bad press. The word does not conjure up a very positive image in the minds of most people. It does make us think, however, of one stalwart

American original, admirable at least for her zeal: Carrie Nation. Old Carrie was a great temperance apostle who would arrive at a gin mill or a brewery with an axe, smash up the place, and break everything in sight. We could use a Carrie Nation today in the pro-life movement — not to advocate destruction of property, but to arouse public indignation in the face of the evil of abortion. People complain about protests in our time, but when Carrie Nation set out to correct a vice, it was like the Last Judgment.

The temperance movement, which actually proposed complete abstinence from any alcoholic beverage, had its gentle apostles too. When the British government encouraged the widespread use of alcohol in subjected Ireland, a remarkable Capuchin friar, Father Matthew, preached total abstinence and gave the "pledge" to millions, preparing the way for Irish independence. His motto was "Ireland sober is Ireland free." There are monuments to him even today in Ireland. An impressive statue, along with monuments to Daniel O'Connell and other Irish heroes, can be seen on O'Connell Street in Dublin. One hopes that the statue will survive the widespread apostasy and secularization of that country, which gave tens of millions a strong faith.

Temperance has never been a popular virtue, although, since it is a natural virtue, it continues on in other movements like dieting and the use of health foods, and in organized programs to control smoking, alcohol, and narcotics.

The natural virtue of temperance simply helps us to use the attractive things of life in a way that contributes to our legitimate goals in life. People can be very temperate agnostics or atheists because they believe that this life is all they have. Oddly enough, believers are often less temperate than others because they believe they are moving on to greener pastures anyway. The addict may console himself with the thought that something better is coming after this life, so why worry about health. Even temperate religious people usually know how to have a good feast, and they often do it in connection with great religious festivals during the year, even if those who are feasting have little grasp of the feast's origin — like Christmas and Easter.

Hilaire Belloc has summed up at least one Catholic attitude toward feast and food:

> Wherever the Catholic sun doth shine,
> There's always laughter and good red wine.
> At least I've always found it so.
> *Benedicamus Domino!*

Supernatural Temperance

A CERTAIN ENJOYMENT of things is compatible with organized religion, including Christianity. All world religions seem to have feasts, and at the same time they all value temperance and even physical mortification. We recall that Our Lord's first miracle was to change water into (very good) wine (see John 2), and of course one of His most notable miracles was the multiplication of loaves and fish to feed thousands. Along with Christ's miracles goes His teaching on moderation and the love of God. According to the Gospel, we must love the Lord our God with all our heart, soul, mind, and strength, and our neighbor as ourselves. There is a comprehensiveness to the commandment, indicating that in all things, including the

> In all things, including the indulgence of appetites, we must be directed toward the kingdom of heaven.

indulgence of appetites, we must be directed toward the kingdom of heaven.

In Christianity, the Gospels, the saints, and the Church Fathers tell us that pleasurable things in life must be directed toward our salvation and the salvation of others. Whatever we enjoy in life should be proportioned and moderated by our spiritual goals. For example, the exchange of sexuality in marriage is a good thing, a creation of God, but it can be misused. Sexuality is a powerful force, and it has an imperative to it; consequently, temperance applies to sexuality, and the virtue of chastity in one's state of life is part of the supernatural virtue of temperance. It is worth noting that when Pope John Paul II reminded married couples about a kind of temperance in legitimate sexual relations, he was ridiculed by the media.

The Abuse of Nature

WE ABUSE MANY THINGS in our society, including the environment. The environmentalists are right. We cause a lot of damage with pesticides and chemical fertilizers. We often would do better to leave nature alone, but we exploit it in order to indulge our intemperance. Far from using the things of the earth abstemiously, we have a tradition of wasting things.

We Americans have too much, and we are not particularly good stewards of what we have.

At a testimonial dinner I once attended, a great deal of food was wasted, including fresh salmon, which is very expensive and very healthful. I eat salmon as often as possible because of the benefits for my heart. I am aware, however, that nature has expended much to produce this elegant dish, and that the salmon has traveled thousands of miles in the sea just to get to my plate. We Americans waste a lot of food, and the virtue of temperance reminds us to be aware of how we use, or abuse, food, which is a gift from God.

We Americans have too much, and we are not particularly good stewards of what we have. We have forgotten, both on a natural level and especially on a supernatural level, that everything should be used for the kingdom of God.

Alexis de Tocqueville, famous for his nineteenth-century observations on the United States, wondered what Americans would do with all the material things with which they were blessed. "What will you do with these things?" he asked. In those days, half the United States was virgin forest. There were vast deposits of minerals that no one had ever touched. What have we done with these things? We have too much, and we don't put it to good use. We should all look at the things in our lives and see whether there is excess.

Common Sense and Temperance

PART OF TEMPERANCE is taking care of ourselves. Obsessive-compulsive workaholism is obviously not a sign of temperance. Even if we enjoy our work, we need to practice temperance and get adequate rest. Careful, Benedict!

Enjoy what's going on while it's going on. If you go to the supermarket, enjoy it. Don't make it drudgery. Talk to the cashier. Speak to the people at the fruit counter. Chat with a neighbor. Try to get to know people, get them to talk to you, and make your passage through life pleasurable. If you are a private person and find it a chore or somewhat difficult to speak to strangers, at least smile. As an old extrovert, I deeply appreciate a quiet person with a genuine smile; in addition, such a person listens to us, which practically no one else does.

Slow down. Smell the flowers as you go by, and then you won't need too much of this world's goods. Enjoy your work and you won't need too much time off. Enjoy being at home and you won't have to go away so much.

> **Many people are intemperate because they are miserable and suffering.**

Many people are intemperate because they are miserable and suffering. Their life is a big long misery, so they decide to brighten it up with mountains of potato chips. They're addicted to potato chips or sweets or even beer. Look at your own intemperateness and see if unhappiness is causing it.

Twelve-Step Programs

I WOULDN'T WANT TO TALK about temperance and not mention the twelve-step programs, which cover every human addiction imaginable. An addiction is a pleasure-producing, self-destructive, irresistible urge or habit. It is always self-destructive, and many people find addictive elements in their personality. They may have learned addictive behavior at home as children. They may even have impulses to self-destruction from their physical makeup. A twelve-step program is often the way to a deep spiritual life. It is worth noting that an addictive impulse can transfer from one substance to another; for example, people sometimes move from alcohol to drug addiction.

Those who, by God's grace, have never experienced a serious addiction may not understand what an addict endures or what a recovering addict may have accomplished by God's grace. We are often too quick to judge others when we do not understand that addicts who are struggling to recover need help and encouragement.

There are people who help addicts, especially relatives, by encouragement or by joining twelve-step movements. Alcoholics Anonymous, the grandfather of all twelve-step programs, has also given rise to programs for relatives and friends of addicts, like Al-Anon. Someone once told me that I would have made a great alcoholic if I had ever got started. I thought about it and decided that I belonged to a huge, unrecognized group of humanity that might be called Alaschleps. The old Yiddish word *schlep*, which derives from the German word for plodder, describes most of us in some aspects of our lives. Alaschleps are people who would have been great alcoholics but who never got started. The Alaschlep motto is: We could not find the bottle opener.

Temperance and Money

THE UNITED STATES and many other countries have become surprisingly affluent. The massive amount of money in these countries is not justly or evenly distributed. This puts a responsibility on those who get or make a lot of money. Money represents the goods of this world, which God intends for the use of all.

It has long been a custom in the United States that the wealthy do things for the good of others and of the country. Many churches, schools, and hospitals have been built by wealthy people. Libraries around the world often bear the name of Andrew Carnegie, who did not hesitate to use his wealth for good. Similarly, museums have traditionally received the benefactions of the rich.

In our country and in others, some people have become extraordinarily wealthy. Many others are far better off today than their parents were. The responsibility then becomes not only to be generous but also to be temperate. The devout Christian should never be extravagant in lifestyle or in personal expenditure. Obviously, money does not buy happiness; it buys comfort. Any family would like to have a reasonable amount of comfort for themselves and their children. One must be very careful, however, with extravagance, which can never be part of Christian life. It can never be justified. This is something about which both Church leaders and Church members need to examine their consciences. Pious extravagance, even in religious objects, is neither admirable nor virtuous. In the past, Catholic immigrants, trying to show that they had really "arrived" in the United States, often indulged in pious extravagances. Bishops wore jeweled crosses, and priests drove fancy cars, practices which clearly went against the Gospel, although those involved may have thought they were doing nothing inappropriate.

The difficult times for the Church right now afford us a wonderful opportunity not only to practice temperance but also to avoid extravagance. We should be extravagantly helpful to the poor, both at home and in the Third World.

Any two or three consecutive pages in the Gospel will point out the necessity of temperance and generosity, especially to the unfortunate. It is something timely for Americans just now, because sooner or later the bubble of great prosperity will break and intemperance will return to haunt its practitioners.

In order to understand Christian temperance, we must constantly recall the humble life of our Lord Jesus Christ and what He chose for Himself. He chose to be born in a little hamlet in a rural part of an occupied country. He lived His whole life in poverty, and He died the death of a poor man. Crucifixion was reserved for the poor and helpless. When we look at the Cross, we must always remember that the One who carried it was the Poor Man of Nazareth.

Most of the time when we talk about intemperance, we are talking about people with problems stemming from addictive behavior. The rest of us can be generally intemperate.

Christian temperance is a virtue that causes us to use all pleasurable or delightful things in such a way that they contribute to our own sanctification and the sanctification of others. It doesn't mean being miserable, but it does mean using the things of this world wisely and well. And when we have too much, we should give it away. That is not charity. Charity is when you give away what you need. Giving away what you don't need is benevolence. Most decent people are benevolent. How many are likely to go without what they need and gave the money away? That's charity. Families often have to do this.

> **The devout Christian should never be extravagant in lifestyle or in personal expenditure.**

Cardinal Newman expressed the Christian ideal this way:

> To be Christians, surely it is not enough to be that which we are enjoined to be, and must be, even without Christ; not enough to be no better than good heathens; not enough to be, in some slight measure, just, honest, temperate, and religious. We must indeed be just, honest, temperate, and religious, before we can rise to Christian graces, and to be practiced in justice and the like virtues is the way, the ordinary way, in which we receive the fulness of the kingdom of God. . . .
>
> It is much more than honesty, justice, and temperance; and this is to be a Christian. . . .
>
> We must have a deep sense of our guilt, and of the difficulty of securing heaven; we must live as in His

presence, daily pleading His cross and passion, think-ing of His holy commandments, imitating His sinless pattern, and depending on the gracious aids of His Spirit; that we may really and truly be servants of Father, Son, and Holy Ghost, in whose name we were baptized. Further, we must, for His sake, aim at a noble and unusual strictness of life, perfecting holiness in His fear, destroying our sins, mastering our whole soul, and bringing it into captivity to His law, denying ourselves lawful things, in order to do Him service, exercising a profound humility, and an unbounded, never-failing love, giving away much of our substance in religious and charitable works, and discountenanc-ing and shunning irreligious men. This is to be a Christian; a gift easily described, and in a few words, but attainable only with fear and much trembling.[28]

Temperance and Generosity

TEMPERANCE IS NOT an elective procedure. It's required by the Gospel.

The Son of Man had no place to lay His head. He chose to live a poor life for us. Jesus called those around Him to a great generosity, to a radical living of poverty. He praised the widow in the Temple who gave all she had to live on. I know a number of wealthy people who have been extremely gener-ous, giving away not only their wealth but also their most pre-cious commodity — their time. Some poor people, on other hand, are absolutely stingy. Some people go to church but are not moved to do something for others. How long will their purgatory be? They will have a lot to learn, because almsgiving is a requirement in both Old and New Testaments. Giving money is a big help and often a sacrifice, but people can also be called to collect and prepare food, work with the homeless, and give their time and effort in other ways.

Saint Vincent de Paul said that if you love the poor, your life will be filled with sunlight and you will not be frightened at the hour of death. I have been blessed to work with poor people since I was eighteen, and I have learned much more from them than I ever taught them. As I look down the road to my death, I'm not the slightest bit frightened. Saint Vincent was right.

Questions for Meditation on Temperance

1. How should we view all created goods? What is their purpose?
2. How is the *Catechism's* definition of temperance (see beginning of the chapter) illustrated by the examples given in this chapter?
3. What place does extravagance have in the life of a follower of Christ? What types of extravagance are highlighted in this chapter?
4. What concrete steps can you take to practice the virtue of temperance? What areas of your life merit special attention?

Prayer

O Lord Jesus Christ, teach me to use all the things of this life and this world for Your kingdom. Whatever I need or enjoy, whatever things I use in the brief time of life, help me always to use them for Your honor and glory and for the betterment of others. Remind me always that we are passing through this world, and that our ownership of things is very temporary — almost an illusion. Help me to curb my needs and appetites so that I will be more prepared to give up things for Your honor and glory and for the needs of my neighbor. I ask this of You, Christ my Lord. Amen.

PART II

The Theological Virtues

Faith

Hope

Charity

The theological virtues are the foundation of Christian moral activity; they animate it and give it its special character. They inform and give life to all the moral virtues. They are infused by God into the souls of the faithful to make them capable of acting as his children and of meriting eternal life. They are the pledge of the presence and action of the Holy Spirit in the faculties of the human being.

— CATECHISM OF THE CATHOLIC CHURCH (N. 1813)

CHAPTER 5

Faith

Jesus answered them, "Have faith in God."

— MARK 11:22

Faith *is the theological virtue by which we believe in God and believe all that he has said and revealed to us, and that Holy Church proposes for our belief, because he is truth itself. By faith "man freely commits his entire self to God"* (Dei Verbum, *n. 5). For this reason the believer seeks to know and do God's will. "The righteous shall live by faith." Living faith "work[s] through charity" (Romans 1:17; Galatians 5:6).*

— CATECHISM OF THE CATHOLIC CHURCH (N. 1814)

UP TO NOW we have been considering the moral virtues, sometimes known as the cardinal virtues.[29] These are good qualities of nature, which in the life of a person in grace are infused by the Holy Spirit and lifted to a higher plane. The natural virtue of prudence, for example, by which we govern our lives so that they will be peaceful and happy, can be changed into the supernatural virtue of prudence, by which we govern our lives so that we may be saved. The same may be said of the other moral virtues. This is not true, however, of the three theological virtues: faith, hope, and charity. They do not have a foundation in human nature, although certain qualities of personality may lead someone to possess one or another of these virtues. Ultimately, they are gifts of God, and we cannot attain them without grace or, after a while, without the free acceptance of grace.

Faith enables us to believe the truths revealed by God about Himself. We could never know these truths on our own, since they transcend the power of human reason. They are exciting and mysterious things: God knows us, which is an article of faith; God created the world out of nothing — it was not always there; God spoke to His people, the Jews; God promised a Messiah, a Savior; God became man in the Person of Jesus Christ; Christ worked miracles; Christ rose from the dead; He will come again.

All these things are truths of faith. They cannot be proven, except by arguments from faith — that is, from revelation. It can be proven by history, for instance, that much of the world was waiting for a Messiah before Christ came, but it was only after He had come that He was revealed as the Son of God.

Faith is very important today in the world and in the Church because many people say they have lost their faith or are not sure of faith.

Faith is very important today in the world and in the Church because many people say they have lost their faith or are not sure of faith. Some are not sure whether they ever had faith; others believe but inconsistently. Nearly every family today has one or more members who have apparently lost their faith. We can lose grace without losing faith. A person can be living in a state of sin but still believe. Father Faber said that faith is so powerful that it preaches even in the darkness of sin.[30]

On the other hand, there are people who once apparently had a great deal of faith but who become indifferent or hostile to faith. During the Spanish Civil War, a woman known as La Pasionaria ("the passionate one"), who was once a leader in Catholic action, became a communist and a profound enemy of the faith. It is said that she violently persecuted the Church, and even killed priests with her bare hands.

What Is Christian Faith?

FAITH IS SAYING yes to God with our mind. Often we say yes to God with our will. If we think God wants us to do a certain thing, we roll up our sleeves, try to do it, and persevere even through failure. That is being faithful and consenting with the mind and will.

Faith begins to exist in the mind and thought process. However, it does not just exist in the mind; we have to make an act of the will to say yes to faith. When we look out the window at the morning sun, we do not have to make an act of faith that the sun is out. We simply have to accept the evidence of our senses. In the psychology of perception, a generally held theory maintains that putting the experience of the senses together into a comprehensible whole takes a kind of decision, which we make spontaneously as do all living creatures around us. However, once in a while we meet someone in a hospital who is in a trance-like state and cannot put everything together.

Once we have looked out the window and decided that the sun is out, we move on without what could be called faith. We simply accept things as they are. Human faith, on the other hand, is believing a message someone has given, which is unknown from personal experience. If a stockbroker advises someone to hold on to his stock and not sell, he will probably put human faith in what the broker says. The same is true if we try a new restaurant based solely on someone's recommendation. We are more likely to believe some people than others. If someone walks up to you on the street and says, "You know, I've got a great deal on stock. Why don't you sell what you have and invest with me," we are not going to believe him. That is what we will call *natural faith* or the denial of natural faith and credibility.

What are we to think of *supernatural faith* or the theological virtue of faith? Cardinal Newman writes:

> Faith . . . is assenting to a doctrine as true, which we do not see, which we cannot prove, because God says it is true, who cannot lie. And further than this, since God says it is true, not with His own voice, but by the voice of His messengers, it is assenting to what man says, not simply viewed as a man, but to what he is commissioned to declare, as a messenger, prophet, or ambassador from God.[31]

Ordinarily, we consider things true because we see them or we can determine with our mind that they exist: for example, we hear someone whom we cannot see knock at the door. We gain truth by sight or by reason of the mind. Because we have never seen God, however, it is necessary to believe His messengers, although we must be cautiously prudent. If someone runs down the street and says, "The Messiah is coming," we are unlikely to believe it.

We have some interesting decisions to make when we are trying to learn about God. We have to ask ourselves about the credibility of witnesses; once we have established their credibility, we have to put our faith in what they say. Once we accept what the messenger of God says and we decide it is the truth, we have to move from human faith in the messenger to divine faith. It does not matter whether it is a question of the authenticity of the Gospels or the consistency of a papal teaching with Sacred Scripture.

Newman writes:

> He who believes that God is true, and that this is His word, which He has committed to man, has no doubt at all. He is as certain that the doctrine taught is true, as that God is true; and he is certain, because God is true, because God has spoken, not because he sees its truth or can prove its truth. That is, faith has two peculiarities; — it is most certain, decided, positive, immovable in its assent, and it gives this assent not because it sees with eye, or sees with the reason, but because it receives the tidings from one who comes from God.[32]

This is what distinguishes faith from other believable things or credibility. True Christian faith, true supernatural faith, is absolute.

When I was a boy, my grandmother used to say, "You'd argue with God." As I got older, I decided I would not do that. I would argue with anybody else, but not with God. I have come to the conclusion that life and the world we live in are very confusing. I can come to some understanding of life only by accepting God. God is a mystery, however, so there is much we cannot understand.

When we look at a realistic crucifix that shows a man in agony and death, we see about Him a great dignity, an aura of great holiness. Nonetheless, He is dying in agony. Blood pours from His arms, palms, and feet. Can this be God? We believe the crucifix is an image of the death of the Son of God, that it really took place, but we cannot entirely understand it.

Faith Is a Gift

THIS BRINGS US TO the second important point about the virtue of faith: It is a gift. We can do nothing in the realm of the supernatural without God's grace. Faith is many things at the same time: assent to the truth of a witness of God, assent to a mysterious truth because even the witness cannot explain everything about God, and a gift enabling us to accept the mystery that the witness brings. Faith is not our own act, which we are free to exert at will. It is different from the exercise of reason, although for Catholics and some other Christian believers, faith can follow from reason.

Some religions like to believe that faith is totally absurd. Martin Luther had said, "I believe because it is absurd." That would not be a particularly Catholic sentiment. In his epistle to the Romans, Saint Paul uses cogent arguments to bring people to the threshold of faith. He condemns the pagans because they did not believe in God from the evidence of their senses and the things around them. Consequently, the Catholic Church has always taught that we should believe so that we can understand and use our reason in order to come to the threshold of belief.

> I would suggest to those who want to believe or think they ought to believe, but do not, to see whether they might unconsciously be placing obstacles in the way of belief.

It is not always necessary to do that. There is a childlike faith of those who believe simply without reason. For an adult, however, faith, although going beyond reason, should not fly in the face of reason, which is also a gift of God. Like all of God's gifts, our intellect can be unruly because of our fallen human nature. It can challenge faith. It can set itself up as a false god. Reason ought to help us make conclusions from Sacred Scripture, without which we would not arrive at the articles of faith. Reason can also be the preamble to faith, taking the soul step by step to belief.

Trying to explain why faith is different from reason, Newman says:

> I may feel the force of the argument for the divine origin of the Church; I may see that I ought to believe; and yet I may be unable to believe. This is no imaginary case; there is many a man who has ground enough to believe, who wishes to believe, but who cannot believe. It is always indeed his own fault, for God gives grace to all who ask for it, and use it, but still such is the fact, that conviction is not faith. . . .[33]

> There are, to be sure, many cogent arguments to lead one to join the Catholic Church, but they do not force the will. We may know them, and not be moved to act upon them. We may be convinced without being persuaded. The two things are quite distinct from each other, seeing you ought to believe, and believing; reason, if left to itself, will bring you to the conclusion that you have sufficient grounds for believing, but belief is the gift of grace. You are then what you are, not from any excellence or merit of your own, but by the grace of God who has chosen you to believe.[34]

This is a mystery. Many people stand quietly around the edges of the Church all their lives. Sometimes they come in at the hour of death. Others skate around forever. Some express real regret that they cannot believe. The great physicist Dr. Robert Jastrow has called himself an agnostic.[35] If I knew Dr. Jastrow, I would suggest that he quietly go off on retreat and pray, just pray. He might say, "I'm not sure I'd know who to pray to." Agnostics should pray anyway. Pray in the subjunctive. "God, if You're there, listen to me." I would also suggest to those who want to believe or think they ought to believe, but do not, to see whether they might unconsciously be placing obstacles in the way of belief. Do they advance reasons why they ought not to believe, because belief would be too inconvenient or too challenging?

Half-Baked Faith

THERE ARE MANY half-baked believers at this time. They sort of believe. This is really a symptom of a loss of faith. As children they may have gone to Catholic school or religious instruction, accepting faith with a good deal of unquestioning belief. This is the faith of children. In adolescence, they found out that many people do not believe. Still, our half-baked believers held on. Perhaps they embraced a religious vocation or the priesthood, or were simply practicing lay Catholics. They were married in the Church and sent their children to Catholic school, but in the back of their minds doubt began to develop. They fell into the temptation of believing some truths and rejecting others. Perhaps they began to doubt that Jesus Christ is equal to the Father, that He is equally God. The Incarnation and the divinity of Christ were hard for them to swallow. After all, He was crucified. How can God be crucified and die? So they think, "Well, the Church almost got it right, but Jesus really isn't equal to God." Perhaps someone told them, "You know, they got very excited in the early Church when the apostles saw — or thought they saw — the risen Christ. Actually, He really rose only spiritually. He came to them after He was dead, but it wouldn't bother me one little bit if they found His skeleton in a tomb. That wouldn't shake my faith at all."

Suddenly, the Resurrection becomes something intellectual, a kind of mystical apparition of Christ after His death. It becomes something like the apparitions at Lourdes, which did not require a good deal of personal subjective conviction. The faith of our already shaky, half-baked believers is further eroded when they hear that the apostles thought Christ rose from the dead because they wanted Him to rise from the dead. It was merely a case of wishful thinking, a kind of self-fulfilling prophecy. If that were the case, we have to ask, "What about the Holy Eucharist? If Christ did not rise from the dead, how could we have His body?" It is not really His body, the skeptics say. After all, that would be ridiculous. It's a symbol. And if it is a symbol, why do we need priests? We can all do it. And so, without much fuss, we have catholic Protestants.

I have lots of good Protestant friends with strong faith. I think some of their faith is erroneously directed, but catholic Protestants are a contradiction. This alarming state of affairs was seen in the number of people who actually accepted the lies and distortions of the *Da Vinci Code* (book or movie) and did not realize that this tissue of lies was also an attack on their faith and a blasphemy against our Lord Jesus Christ.

Many people are in this category today. Their faith is weak and dying. They have refused to believe the Gospel and its witnesses. Their faith is caught at an adolescent stage and has not moved on to adult faith, which accepts God without hesitation. Even for those living in sin, mature faith may be possible. They may lose it rather easily, but they could truly believe and even tremble because they know that their eternal salvation is in jeopardy.

Again, Newman writes, on submission in faith:

> I come then to this conclusion; — if I must submit my reason to mysteries, it is not much matter whether it is a mystery more or a mystery less, when faith anyhow is the very essence of all religion, when the main difficulty to an inquirer is firmly to hold that there is a Living God, in spite of the darkness which surrounds Him, the Creator, Witness, and Judge of men. When once the mind is broken in, as it must be, to the belief of a Power above it, when once it understands, that it is not itself the measure of all things in heaven and earth, it will have little difficulty in going forward. I do not say it will, or can, go on to other truths, without conviction; I do not say it ought to believe the Catholic faith without grounds and motives; but I say that, when once it believes in God, the great obstacle to faith has been taken away, — a proud, self-sufficient spirit. When once a man really, with the eyes of his soul and by the power of Divine grace, recognizes his Creator, he has passed a line; that has happened to him which cannot happen twice; he has bent his stiff neck, and triumphed over himself.[36]

It is my impression that many people today do not reach this point. They arrive at an unspecified religious opinion. Human beings have a natural need to believe in God, which, as we have seen, is called the virtue of religion and is part of the virtue of justice. It is not really supernatural faith, and this kind of religiosity can masquerade as lukewarm Catholicism. We have all met people, even those who appear to speak in the name of religion, who may not have strong personal faith. Their faith is weak, half-baked, irresolute, and they are unconvincing to anybody else, because faith is a response — a response as strong or weak as we choose to make it.

If we really believe, we will pray to God every day. It will be important to pray to Him, speak to Him, and ask for His help. We will enjoy and be fed by meditating on His mysteries. We will do what He said and have a spirit of self-sacrifice. Our priorities will be to seek, listen, struggle, search, find, do, go beyond the commonplace, and be better and more religious than a decent unbeliever, who may also have a measure of prudence, justice, fortitude, and temperance. If we are unwilling to go beyond an elementary level of faith, it will begin to slip away, and it will become easy to accept this and reject that.

The Great Act of Faith

THE GREATEST ARTICLE of faith of Christianity is the divinity of Christ. This is what separates Christians from other believers in the one true God, like Moslems and Jews and others who seek a Messiah. In *Crossing the Threshold of Hope*, Pope John Paul II wrote:

> This Church professes: "You are the Messiah, the Son of the living God." Over the centuries this has been the Church's profession of faith, as well as that of those who share her faith and of all those to whom the Father revealed the Son in the Holy Spirit, just as the

Son in the Holy Spirit revealed to them the Father (cf. Mt 11:25–27).

This Revelation is *definitive*; one can only accept it or reject it. One can accept it, professing belief in God, the Father Almighty, Creator of heaven and earth, and in Jesus Christ, the Son, of the same substance as the Father and the Holy Spirit, who is Lord and the Giver of life. Or one can reject all of this, writing in capital letters: "God does not have a Son"; "Jesus Christ is not the Son of God, He is only one of the prophets, and even if not the least of them, he is only a man."

How can we marvel at such arguments when we know that Peter himself had difficulties in this respect? He believed in the Son of God, but he was unable to accept that this Son of God, as a man, could be whipped, crowned with thorns, and then had to die on the Cross.

Is it any wonder that even those who believe in one God, of whom Abraham was a witness, find it difficult to have faith in a crucified God? They hold that God can only be powerful and grandiose, absolutely transcendent and beautiful in His power, holy and inaccessible to man. God can only be this! He cannot be the Father, the Son, and the Holy Spirit. He cannot be Love that gives of Himself and that permits that He be seen, that He be heard, that He be imitated as a man, that He be bound, that He be beaten and crucified. This cannot be God! Therefore, at the center of a great tradition of monotheism a *profound division* was introduced.[37]

Among Oriental people, there are many who believe in one true God. Scholars in the nineteenth century deceived people a little, and even Pope John Paul II may have been confused by them. They said that Buddhists are always atheistic, but that is not true. Obviously, they do not believe in the God of Abraham, Isaac, and Jacob, but they certainly may be looking for Him. Many Buddhists believe in and pray to a personal God, as I have seen in Buddhist temples in the Orient.

It takes a good deal of faith to believe that a man who was crucified and who died was and is truly God, but that is the Christian faith and the faith of the Catholic Church. Pope John Paul II continues:

> In the Church — built on the rock that is Christ — Peter, the apostles, and their successors are witnesses of God crucified and risen in Christ. They are witnesses of the life that is stronger than death. They are witnesses of God who gives life because He is Love (cf. 1 Jn 4:8). They are witnesses because they saw, heard, and touched with their hands the eyes and ears of Peter, John, and many others. But Christ said to Thomas: "Blessed are those who have not seen and have believed" (Jn 20:29).[38]

The same truth was emphasized by his successor, Pope Benedict XVI, a few years before his election as pope:

> It must be firmly believed as a truth of Catholic faith that the universal salvific will of the One and Triune God is offered and accomplished once and for all in the mystery of the incarnation, death, and resurrection of the Son of God.[39]

This is the essence of the Christian faith. In these unbelieving times, we have to ask whether we really have faith. Do we show our faith by our behavior and loyalty to the Church of Christ? Loyalty means hanging on when things are not going well. It means that when the Church is attacked or disgraced, we are there for her. It means that when even those who represent the Church appear to vacillate or equivocate with a half-baked faith, we do not imitate them.

Do we show our faith by our behavior and loyalty to the Church of Christ?

One of the most interesting things about faith is that God wants us to believe, He wants us to accept this gift. In the Gospel, Our Lord often complained, "O ye of little faith" (Douay-Rheims). "When the Son of man comes, will he find faith on earth?" (Luke 18:8). He seems to ask almost in a sense of frustration. He calls people to faith. He actually compliments people on their faith, particularly pagans who put their trust in Him when they needed a miraculous cure. He said to the Canaanite woman, "O woman, great is your faith!" (Matthew 15:28).

God not only gives us faith, but He also asks us to believe. It is the very essence of God to share His goodness and His blessings with His children. Christ came into the world, suffered, and died because He wanted us to share in the divine life, which is the very meaning of eternal life. He wants us to be participants with Him in the heavenly kingdom. The first step on the road to that kingdom is faith.

Again Pope John Paul II wrote:

Christ wants to awaken faith in human hearts. He wants them to respond to the word of the Father, but He wants this in full respect for human dignity. In the very search for faith an implicit faith is already present, and therefore the necessary condition for salvation is already satisfied.[40]

This means that there is already a desire on the part of many people to believe. This is recognized by the Church in the Second Vatican Council when it says:

> Those also can attain to salvation who through no fault of their own do not know the Gospel of Christ or His Church, yet sincerely seek God and moved by grace strive by their deeds to do His will as it is known to them through the dictates of conscience. Nor does Divine Providence deny the helps necessary for salvation to those who, without blame on their part, have not yet arrived at an explicit knowledge of God and with His grace strive to live a good life. (*Lumen Gentium*, n. 16)

The Usefulness of Faith

THE USEFULNESS OF FAITH is manifold.

First, the desire for faith among those who sincerely seek God with the help of the grace of Christ can open the door to eternal salvation. No human being can save himself. The only one who can save us is Christ. And we cling to Christ by faith. In the Gospel, Our Lord expects people to believe in Him.

Second, faith is extremely useful in binding together in this fallen world those who believe in God and want to do the right thing. For an individual or a group, for the whole Church, faith indicates the right moral behavior in fulfilling the requirements of the Gospel. Faith is a teacher. Many today reject faith because they do not want to follow its moral teachings. New Agers express a belief in a divine being, a transcendent being, but they are frequently unwilling to accept the total objective morality demanded by the Gospel and divine revelation. I do not say that they are necessarily immoral, but they tend very much to pick and choose, and they do so with complete peace of mind. Christians who pick and choose will know in the depths of their heart that they are doing wrong, but the New Age disciple will not have any awareness of this. Therefore, they are led astray.

Faith is also extremely useful in helping us survive this life. When a tragedy befalls someone, how often do we say, "How can anyone survive this without faith?" Faith is a constant and firm support, even in the darkest times. When terrible calamities have happened to me, as when I awoke three weeks after being hit by a car, I went through a period of shock and did not know what to do. I felt that God was far away, and doubts came to mind. However, I found that after struggling with the darkness a day or two, faith began to shine again brightly. Then I wondered how I was ever so shaken. I have come to believe that the sense of what amounts almost to desperation is an equivalent to what our Divine Savior went through in the Garden of Gethsemane. On the other hand, the return of faith is almost like a mini-resurrection. Saint Paul says, "I can do all things in him who strengthens me" (Philippians 4:13). How do we get to Him who strengthens us if not by faith?

Saint Paul was the apostle who cherished faith the most. He had come to faith the hard way, having been confronted by the risen Christ Himself on the road to Damascus. It is difficult to characterize Saint Paul as a theologian of this or that because his entire presentation of Christianity is so complete. There's hardly anything he does not cover. He might be called the Christian theologian of faith. The epistle to the Romans — especially chapters 3, 4, and 5 — is a powerful expression of faith. Obviously, Saint Paul did not think that faith was the only source of salvation. In the first epistle to the Corinthians, he says that charity is the greatest of the theological virtues, but we cannot get to charity without faith. "So faith, hope, love abide, these three; but the greatest of these is love" (1 Corinthians 13:13). However, we never get to love unless the door is opened by faith. He also says that the virtuous man lives by faith. This is a powerful insight for our own time, which erroneously thinks that the virtuous man lives by a generalized kindliness. It may not even be Christian virtue. It may be simply an attitude of humanity, or living according to one's opinions or those of others, or by good works. The virtuous man, however, lives by faith, is taught by faith, and knows what to do by faith. Faith is what guides him.

A Man of Great Faith

I OCCASIONALLY OFFER MASS at a Chinese Catholic Church in Santa Clara, California. It is on the property of the old mission of Santa Clara, founded by Father Junípero Serra and now in the care of the Jesuit Fathers. I was deeply moved by the faith of the Chinese people, whose devotion and reverence at Mass seemed to indicate that they knew from personal experience what it is like to be persecuted. I met a Chinese Jesuit, Father George Wong, who had been a prisoner for fifteen years and then was forced to work on a labor farm for another fifteen, all for the crime of being a Catholic priest.

He was a very gentle man. It would have been understandable if he had been enraged or angry or hurt, or if he had not readjusted to society outside the prison after thirty years. But Father Wong spoke about his experiences with candor, humor, and a sense that he was being led by God during that time. He even described how he had been handcuffed with his hands behind his back for fifty days for teaching someone the Hail Mary. He said he did not quite know how he had survived, but he had never lost his faith. He had prayed. He had said the prayers of the Mass. He had remained loyal. It was all so matter-of-fact and taken so much in stride that one had to stop and realize what this man had been through.

As I thought later about my meeting with him, I realized that I had been in the presence of something very powerful but also very quiet — namely, his great faith. Saint John says it very well: "This is the victory that overcomes the world, our faith" (1 John 5:4). Certainly our troubled world, with its scandals and undermining of religious belief, needs faith more than anything else. Faith opens the door to God's mercy and guidance. With faith we rely on Divine Providence even in the worst of circumstances. We have hope in eternal life. Above all, faith enables us to see Christ in the people around us, especially those who are needy and poor.

The Gospels record many incidents of Our Lord performing cures as a result of someone's faith, as for example in the case of the woman cured of a hemorrhage:

Jesus turned, and seeing her he said, "Take heart, daughter; your faith has made you well." And instantly the woman was made well. (Matthew 9:22)

Or the case of blind Bartimaeus:

And Jesus said to him, "What do you want me to do for you?" And the blind man said to him, "Master, let me receive my sight." And Jesus said to him, "Go your way; your faith has made you well." And immediately he received his sight and followed him on the way. (Mark 10:51–52)

We should always approach God with faith. We should see life and its troubles with the eyes of faith. Faith opens the door to salvation, so in this sense we are saved by faith and hope, as Saint Paul teaches. But, according to him, we must move on to charity.

Questions for Meditation on Faith

1. What type of faith do you have?
2. What steps can you take to embrace all that God has revealed and continues to propose through the Church's Magisterium?
3. How do your daily actions and words reflect your faith in God and His Church?
4. How can you live by faith more in the future?

Prayer

Holy Spirit, come to me and increase my faith. Raise me beyond my confusion and doubts and give me an inner vision of truth and Your divine light. We cannot believe without You, so give me the courage to surrender to You.

Your mysteries are beyond the comprehension of my mind, but they are not beyond the acceptance of my will. Give me, then, O Lord, the grace to open my mind and heart to You. Then I shall believe, and my belief shall guide me in all the events of life. In whatever way Your providence provides, I shall be most desirous to share my faith in Christ with others in the most effective way. Amen.

CHAPTER 6

Hope

◈━━━━━◈

Let us hold fast the confession of our hope without wavering, for he who promised is faithful.

— HEBREWS 10:23

Hope is the theological virtue by which we desire the kingdom of heaven and eternal life as our happiness, placing our trust in Christ's promises and relying not on our own strength, but on the help of the grace of the Holy Spirit.... "The Holy Spirit... [is] poured out upon us richly through Jesus Christ our Savior, so that we might be justified by his grace and become heirs in hope of eternal life" (Titus 3:6–7).

— CATECHISM OF THE CATHOLIC CHURCH (N. 1817)

IS THERE A MORE BEAUTIFUL word than *hope*? Many people, however, are disappointed when they do not get what they hoped for, so we should make a few distinctions. Christians cannot be absolute optimists, because we know from Scripture and Church teaching that some people go to hell. Some things are not going to work out in the end. Nor can Christians be absolute pessimists, because many people — perhaps the great majority — with the grace of God are pushed, shoved, dragged, or cajoled into eternal life. So the extremes of either position are to be avoided.

Many Christian preachers go around telling everyone that everything is going to work out beautifully. Presumably, if we think everything is going to work out beautifully, life will go very well. Perhaps the most determined disciple of positive thinking was Norman Vincent Peale. In an interview on his ninetieth birthday, Dr. Peale said: "I've lived all my life in misery, but I decided not to let it get me down." If that admission had come out before, I would have been more positively disposed to him than I was. Being a moderate pessimist, I become rather annoyed with those who are certain that only the best will happen. My generation did not expect the best to happen. We were delighted when the worst did not happen. Perhaps this attitude is related to courage.

> We may come to a situation one day when a doctor will say, "There is no hope." That's when the Christian virtue of hope must be practiced.

Holy Hope

What about the theological virtue of hope? It has only one object: salvation — for oneself, for those dear to us, and for the world. That is why we can have hope when everything seems hopeless. The beautiful Protestant hymn "Abide With Me" is the prayer of a dying soul filled with hope. We may come to a situation one day when a doctor will say, "There is no hope." That's when the Christian virtue of hope must be practiced. Saint Paul says that we have hope in spite of hope, meaning both theological hope and human hope.

The theological virtue of hope helps us organize our lives and put up with the difficulties and sufferings of life, and even of death. It convinces us that in the mighty hands of God and through the Precious Blood of our Lord Jesus Christ we will receive in abundance and forever all the good things that we have aspired to in this world, and that we will go completely beyond them in the kingdom of God. I think perhaps you practice hope most if you live through a lot of apparently hopeless situations. Green is the color of hope. It is used in Church most often in Ordinary Time — the period exclusive of Advent–Christmastide and Lent–Eastertide. It is the color of spring and symbolizes renewed life.

The Catholic poet Charles Péguy, who led a difficult life and died in World War I, wrote a beautiful poem about the virtues, in which the speaker is God the Father. Concerning hope, he says, "Ah, hope, my little daughter, my little girl running on and playing in front of me in the world. Little hope, so fragile, so frail, but she's always there."

In the affluent suburbs of big cities like New York, pessimism is not an attitude but a way of life. People look incredibly depressed, and of course to be upwardly mobile is to admit that you know that life is empty and hollow. After people arrive at the promised land where milk and honey flow, they realize it is not so wonderful. One psychological study has indicated that in affluent suburbs at least two-thirds of the population are in some kind of therapy. It may be masquerading as spiritual direction or something else, but many are hoping to get some kind of help. If you really want to have a lot of fun and see people enjoying it, go to a block party on 156th Street in the Bronx. Watch kids throwing water balloons at one another from the top of five-story tenements and having a marvelous time.

In *Crossing the Threshold of Hope*, Pope John Paul II tells us that the Enlightenment and science have not found the promised land. The Founding Fathers thought America was going to be the promised land of the Enlightenment. The Protestants who were largely responsible for setting up the United States thought that it was going to be Zion, a New Jerusalem. Catholicism, on the other hand, has traditionally been regarded as unenlightened and unprogressive:

> Catholicism, as it has come down to us from the first, seems to be mean and illiberal; it is a mere popular religion; it is the religion of illiterate ages or servile populations or barbarian warriors; it must be treated with discrimination and delicacy, corrected, softened, improved, if it is to satisfy an enlightened generation. It must be stereotyped as the patron of arts, or the pupil of speculation, or the protégé of science; it must play the literary academician, or the empirical philanthropist, or the political partisan; it must keep up with the age; some or other expedient it must devise, in order to explain away, or to hide, tenets under which the intellect labors and of which it is ashamed — its doctrine, for instance, of grace, its mystery of the Godhead, its preaching of the Cross, its devotion to the Queen of Saints, or its loyalty to the Apostolic See.[41]

Much time, effort, and money have been expended by recent generations of American Catholics, especially in higher education, apologizing for their faith and Church. They have been eager to shed an identity so closely associated with immigrant populations. Much of what was promoted as the "spirit of Vatican II" was an attempt to do this, and many

Catholics gave away their birthright and faith in order to be mainstream — that is, acceptable to the higher echelons of government, academia, and the haut monde. Acceptance was bought at a high price: they lost hope in what they had abandoned, and all hope evaporated from their new aspirations, as the stench of corruption filled the country from these self-destructing institutions.

The children of this world are often wiser in their own generation than are the children of the light, because everything the children of this world believed in went down the drain ninety years ago in the Battle of Verdun. The great humanistic enlightened experiment to make Europe the happy kingdom of the scientifically well-informed came to an end in the First World War. At Verdun, more than three quarters of a million men were killed or wounded. There was not one square inch of turf around the city of Verdun that had not been hit by bombs and blown up.[42] People learned that while scientific progress could make some things better, it could also make others a lot worse.

Some people didn't give up. Two in particular had a desire to make a perfect society, a perfect world free of the mistakes of past history. They were Vladimir Lenin and Adolf Hitler, both of whom saw themselves as benefactors of mankind. Hitler was rather circumscribed in who he thought was going to be capable of being perfect — the Aryans. Lenin thought he could do it by absolute dictatorship. They regressed to a level of barbarism unparalleled since the end of the Roman Empire, and they did it in the name of hope of humanity — a perfect world.

No one is more dangerous than those who set out to make a perfect world. They are sure they have the answer, and they are going to impose it on everyone else. I've lived through messiahs. Psychology, my own field, was going to make everyone happy. In the early days, Freud was thought to have all the answers. Beware of such people and of those who are going to make the world perfect.

> Don't make your belief in God dependent even on pious human hopes, because God works in mysterious ways.

If anyone was going to make a perfect world, it would have been our Blessed Lord. What happened to Him? He was crucified. Do not be taken in by the various messiahs of our age, whether they be people, movements, or trends.

I once said to an old English bishop, "What do you think will be the ultimate outcome?" He looked at me for a moment and said, "The Last Judgment," indicating that we must first put all human hope in perspective. That may mean hope for one's children, business, career, or even the Church. But don't make your belief in God dependent even on pious human hopes, because God works in mysterious ways.

The mother of one of the boys at Children's Village was once arrested for stealing a truck filled with groceries. Following her arrest, she wrote explaining this unpleasant turn of events, saying, "I'll probably be here for six months, but we must remember that the Lord works in mysterious ways, His wonders to perform." That indicated that at least she had some hope. Beyond human hope is eternal hope. We have free will. God did not knock the hammers out of the hands of the executioners at Calvary. He did not move the heart of Pilate to listen to his wife's plea, "Have nothing to do with that righteous man, for I have suffered much over him today in a dream" (Matthew 27:19). Similarly with Judas, the high priest, the leaders of the Sanhedrin, the crowd, and the executioners — all operated with free will. Out of evil freely committed by men God brings good, but this will never be understood unless we look beyond this world and see a heavenly hope. There will be disappointments. Our Lord was disappointed. We call our Blessed Mother "Our Lady of Sorrows," and Our Lord the "Man of Sorrows." Several times He expressed His disappointment and sorrow that both He and His message from the Father were rejected by so many:

> "O faithless and perverse generation, how long am I to be with you? How long am I to bear with you?" (Matthew 17:17)

> "When the Son of man comes, will he find faith on earth?" (Luke 18:8)

> "O Jerusalem, Jerusalem, killing the prophets and stoning those who are sent to you! How often would I have gathered your children together as a hen gathers her brood under her wings, and you would not!" (Matthew 23:37)

The last quote is commemorated in a special way at the chapel of Dominus Flevit ("the Lord wept"), in Jerusalem. It overlooks the city and is built on the site where it is believed Our Lord said those words. On the front of the chapel altar are the words, "Jerusalem, Jerusalem." Between them is a carving of a little hen. Our Lord felt disappointment when He made His lamentation over the city. His hope that the Chosen People would accept His message was dashed. He had a human hope, which came to nothing.

The Ultimate Hope

THEN THERE IS HOPE in eternal life. God must bring down the mountains and fill in the valleys. There must be a hope for the broken, the twisted. There must be hope for the good who have constantly failed — and none of us is perfectly good. We all know that when others fail us, we have probably failed them. There must be something beyond this.

> Our hope in eternal life derives from the promise of someone who experienced the dregs of human suffering.

When I was an altar boy, one of the prayers at the burial service said: "Let them languish not in fruitless and unavailing grief, nor sorrow as those who have no hope." The expression of this hope for the Christian is identified by many saints, and it is clearly identified in *Crossing the Threshold of Hope* in response to the question "Why is there so much evil in the world?"

> Is the God who allows all this still truly Love, as Saint John proclaims in his First Letter? Indeed, is He just with respect to His creatures? Doesn't He place too many burdens on the shoulders of individuals? Doesn't He leave man alone with these burdens, condemning him to a life without hope? So many incurably ill people in hospitals, so many handicapped children, so many human lives completely denied ordinary happiness on this earth, the happiness that comes from love, marriage, and family. All this adds up to a bleak picture, which has found expression in ancient and modern literature. Consider, for example, Fyodor Dostoyevsky, Franz Kafka, or Albert Camus.[43]

Pope John Paul II does not explain the why of suffering; he holds out the example of the scandal of the Cross, citing the Latin proverb: *Stat crux dum volvitur orbis* ("The Cross stands firm while the world turns"):

> Given our present discussion, we must ask ourselves: Could it have been different? Could God have *justified Himself* before human history, so full of suffering, without placing Christ's Cross at the center of that history?

The Cross of Christ is certainly at the center of history, and therefore we have to have our hope in the Cross:

> Obviously, one response could be that God does not need to justify Himself to man. It is enough that He is omnipotent. From this perspective everything He does or allows must be accepted. This is the position of the biblical Job. But God, who besides being Omnipotence is Wisdom and — to repeat once again — Love, desires to justify Himself to mankind. He is not the Absolute that remains outside of the world, indifferent to human suffering. He is Emmanuel, God-with-us, a God who shares man's lot and participates in his destiny. This brings to light another inadequacy, the completely false image of God which the Enlightenment accepted uncritically. With regard to the Gospel, this image certainly represented a step backward, not in the direction of a better knowledge of God and the world, but in the direction of misunderstanding them. . . .

God is not someone who remains only outside of the world, content to be in Himself all-knowing and omnipotent. His *wisdom and omnipotence are placed, by free choice, at the service of creation.* If suffering is present in the history of humanity, one understands why His omnipotence was manifested *in the omnipotence of humiliation on the Cross.* The scandal of the Cross remains the key to the interpretation of the great mystery of suffering, which is so much a part of the history of mankind.

Even contemporary critics of Christianity are in agreement on this point. Even they see that the crucified Christ is *proof of God's solidarity with man in his suffering.*[44]

Therefore, we have hope not simply in eternal life; our hope in eternal life derives from the promise of someone who experienced the dregs of human suffering.

I am very annoyed by the way we in the Church currently play down the crucifixion and death of Jesus Christ. Even our present Good Friday liturgy is a disappointment. People have been cruelly misled today into thinking they can have life without suffering.

You and I have been given the secret of hope. Hope answers the question *what,* not *why.*

No one and nothing can take away our hope — neither failure nor disgrace. One priest I knew whose lifework went up in smoke said to me, "Better to lose this than to lose your soul." He still had hope. If you are looking for a secret to tune all of the discordant notes of life, or something to put it all together, no matter how absurd, preposterous, tragic, or unjust, line it up by the Cross. The Cross should be for the human race the ultimate sign of hopelessness. God sent His Son, and they killed Him. The best God could do they brought down in total failure. His disciples ran away. It was a complete mess. The Cross of Christ is the sign of ultimate defeat of goodness in the world. It is also the sign of ultimate victory. Without the death and resurrection of Christ, hope is brave, admirable. Even those who do not believe in Christ have hope — Jews, Muslims, Hindus, and Buddhists. They hope that something will eventually make sense.

You and I have been given the secret of hope. Hope answers the question *what*, not *why*. What must I do? We receive the bread of hope as often as we wish. Holy Communion is the bread of hope. When we receive it the last time, it will be the absolute bread of hope. It is called Viaticum, the bread to take us through the doors of death.

I once heard a beautiful expression of hope from my dear friend Sister Cuthbert, when she was dying at Marymount. She was a woman of great faith and a true religious. As I said good-bye with a tear in my eye, she said "Oh, Father, don't cry. One of these days our Blessed Mother is going to come and take me home." What people would pay to have that hope! It would be worth millions. Jesus preached hope when He said, "I was hungry and you gave me food, I was thirsty and you gave me drink, I was a stranger and you welcomed me, I was naked and you clothed me" (Matthew 25:35–36).

Here is a prayer of hope from Cardinal Newman's meditations:

O my Lord and Saviour, in Thy arms I am safe; keep me and I have nothing to fear; give me up and I have nothing to hope for. I know not what will come upon me before I die. I know nothing about the future, but

I rely upon Thee. I pray Thee to give me what is good for me; I pray Thee to take from me whatever may imperil my salvation; I pray Thee not to make me rich, I pray Thee not to make me very poor; but I leave it all to Thee, because Thou knowest and I do not. If Thou bringest pain or sorrow on me, give me grace to bear it well — keep me from fretfulness and selfishness. If Thou givest me health and strength and success in this world, keep me ever on my guard lest these great gifts carry me away from Thee. O Thou who didst die on the Cross for me, even for me, sinner as I am, give me to know Thee, to believe on Thee, to love Thee, to serve Thee; ever to aim at setting forth Thy glory; to live to and for Thee; to set a good example to all around me; give me to die just at that time and in that way which is most for Thy glory, and best for my salvation.[45]

When we have that hope, we have the ability to share it with others — with our friends, loved ones, and families. I have no trouble hoping for the salvation for those who seem far away from God, because I know very well where I would be if He dropped me for a single day. I could be an atheist. I could be really nasty because the nastiness is right under the surface. Since He has been so generous to me, I trust that He will be generous to others also. My hope is in the Cross of Jesus Christ. I have seen that hope come to the dying many times.

Juanito Has Hope

WHEN I WAS AT Children's Village, a boy was sent there for picking the pocket of a loan shark. Juanito got $5,000 in $100 bills and gave it away to everybody on the West Side. The cops moved in, got Juanito, the wallet, and the loan shark, who as a result, went upstate as a guest of the government for several years. Juanito was a good-natured fellow. After he went home, he phoned me while I was giving a retreat upstate. His mother had been arrested.

"What did she do?" I asked.

"She's an Avon lady," he said. That's a Puerto Rican answer.

"Why was she arrested as an Avon lady?"

"She was selling marijuana," he told me.

"Juanito, I'm giving a retreat," I said. "Where are the kids?"

"They're with my aunt."

"Hold tight. I'll be down Sunday evening, and Monday morning I'll go to court and I'll get her out."

On Monday morning, I showed up at the house, and there was his mother doing the dishes. "How did you get out of jail?" I asked her.

"Oh," she said, "Juanito took the television set, sold it in the street for fifty dollars, and went down to the courthouse. He hired a lawyer who was standing on the steps, and he got me out for fifty bucks."

He had the presence of mind to do that at the age of fifteen.

Juanito got married to a girl who had been a junkie and who had AIDS. So Juanito had AIDS for five years. He received the sacraments with the unhesitating faith of the very poor and simple. He had unquestioning hope. When he was dying at Saint Vincent's Hospital, I anointed him and gave him Holy Communion. He said to his sister and me, "My life is over. It's coming to an end." Then he raised him arm as if he was trying to catch something.

"Juanito, what are you doing?" his sister asked him.

"Can't you see them?" he said.

"No. What do you see?"

"The angels." He kept reaching out. "Don't you see them? They're coming to get me. My life is over."

As Juanito kept reaching out and smiling, a hush came over his sister and me. There was no doubt that he thought he was seeing angels coming. I was deeply moved. Was it an illusion at the hour of death? Was it real? Did he see such a vision? I cannot say, but I do know that in some real theological way he was right.

One of my confreres buried him because I was away, and the Church put on his lips these words of hope:

> May the angels lead thee into paradise, and may the martyrs come to welcome thee on thy way and bring thee to Jerusalem, the holy city. May the choir of angels welcome thee, and with Lazarus, who was once so poor, may thou have life everlasting.

That's hope.

Questions for Meditation on Hope

1. What does the virtue of hope ultimately desire?
2. How does the virtue of hope hold the key to facing our cross in daily life?
3. What is necessary to ensure that our hope is not in vain?
4. How do the examples in the chapter illustrate the *Catechism*'s definition of hope (cited at the beginning of the chapter)?

Prayer

O Lord Jesus Christ, You came into this world and led a poor and humble life, and then endured an appalling, terrible death. All of this should give us hope, even in the darkest moments. You constantly promised eternal life to those who followed You, and just a few hours before Your death You consoled the apostles, telling them: "Let not your hearts be troubled; believe in God, believe also in me. . . . I go to prepare a place for you" (John 14:1–2).

Increase my hope, O Lord, that I may share it with others, especially when they are in dark times, and never let me be without hope. Purify my hope; let me never place it even in the best of friends, but only and always in You. I pray to You, O Christ my Lord. Amen.

CHAPTER 7

Charity

"As the Father has loved me, so have I loved you; abide in my love. If you keep my commandments, you will abide in my love, just as I have kept my Father's commandments and abide in his love."

— JOHN 15:9–10

Charity is the theological virtue by which we love God above all things for his own sake, and our neighbor as ourselves for the love of God.

Jesus makes charity the new commandment.[46] *By loving his own "to the end" (Jn 13:1), he makes manifest the Father's love which he receives. By loving one another, the disciples imitate the love of Jesus which they themselves receive. Whence Jesus says:... "This is my commandment, that you love one another as I have loved you" (Jn 15:12).*

— CATECHISM OF THE CATHOLIC CHURCH (NN. 1822, 1823)

IN ENGLAND they have an old saying: "There is nothing colder than charity." Outside Catholic circles the word *charity* is sometimes used in a disparaging way. "Oh, they just got charity" or "I won't accept charity." The word fares better among Roman Catholics, perhaps because we have the Sisters of Charity, the Missionaries of Charity, and Catholic Charities.

This reflects the fact that we use the word in a sense that is closer to the Latin *caritas*, which means "love."

However, *love* is an equally ambiguous word. Many terrible things have been done in the name of love — war, murder, etc. The prostitute says to her customer, "Buy some love." The parent who has dominated a child so that he cannot grow says, "But I did it out of love." Oddly, love and hatred often coexist.

Along with faith and hope, charity — or love — is a theological virtue. They are special gifts that God gives so that the soul may be saved. Natural affection can be a natural virtue and, like any other natural virtue, can be lifted to a higher plane — but it is not charity. It does not lead to eternal life.

After I began this book, Pope Benedict XVI issued his first encyclical, *Deus Caritas Est*. This remarkable document, unique in many ways, focuses on the many meanings of love. It should be read in its entirety in a single sitting, which is not difficult. I am tempted to see a synchrony between Pope Benedict's letter and the new emphasis in positive psychology. Put in the terms of psychology, which does not directly explore the Christian concept of charity as a theological virtue, there are many similarities between this virtue and what Peterson and Seligman call humanity and even transcendence.

The most notable differences relate to the love of enemies and personal devotion to God:

> Early Christianity... began to see *agape* as a lavish outpouring of unconditional love by God, in the person of Christ, for all people in need of redemption. As one is forgiven, he or she is directed to forgive (see John's Gospel, chapter 15, as one example).[47]

Pope Benedict adds to our understanding of *eros*, the idea of unity of body and soul. *Eros* itself passes beyond the physical:

Christian faith, on the other hand, has always considered man a unity in duality, a reality in which spirit and
matter compenetrate, and in which each is brought to
a new nobility. True, *eros* tends to rise "in ecstasy"
towards the Divine, to lead us beyond ourselves; yet for
this very reason it calls for a path of ascent, renuncia-
tion, purification and healing.[48]

Those who take the time to read the encyclical will find it
a very creative insight into a virtuous life that is both human
and divine. This is a goal that people have sought for centuries. The popularity of Saint Francis of Assisi, who was at
once filled with sacrificial love and love for the things of the
earth, is probably a testimony to how earnestly people wish to
find a meeting place between *eros* and *agape*.

The word *love* is analyzed in *The Four Loves* by C. S.
Lewis. The author uses four Greek words to describe different
kinds of love: *eros*, *storge*, *philia*, and *agape*. *Eros* is the love that
most people think about exclusive of charity, and it has kind of
a bad name. *Eros* denotes the love we have for something that
fulfills our needs or something we delight in. So the love of
good music or good food is *eros*. What fulfills our needs we love
and cherish — a house, a car, a favorite pet.

Eros

Eros IS ESSENTIALLY self-centered (not necessarily in a negative way), as Pope Benedict has pointed out, because it is based
on the fulfillment of personal needs. There is nothing wrong
with it, but in the realm of personal relationships, especially
marriage, there must be something beyond or the relationship
will not last. *Eros* also gives some kind of fulfillment or plea-

sure to the individual. In English the word is closely associated with the erotic and the sexual and the biological satisfaction of sexual relations, but that is a narrow definition of *eros*. It is a definition, as Pope Benedict pointed out, that leads to the debasement of the human body.

Saint Augustine goes so far as to say that the Christian life is an *eros* for God. The whole of the Christian life is a spiritual *eros*, and he sums this up in one of his most famous statements: "Late have I loved Thee, O beauty so ancient and so new; late have I loved Thee!"

Don't dismiss *eros* from your spiritual life. People are interested in how they can pray better, meaning how they can feel better when they pray. The most fervent prayers are those said in times of dereliction, sorrow, and hopelessness. Perhaps the most intense prayer is said when we get a flat tire in a snowstorm on a deserted country road and we cannot get the lug nuts off the wheel. This prayer is fervent, but it is not *eros*. *Eros* can be fine, but there must be more in our spiritual life, or it will not last. It is a fair-weather friend.

Storge

STORGE IS ONE OF THE most important and effective elements of human existence. It can do immense good or immense evil. In order not to confuse the issue of *eros* and *agape*, I think the Holy Father omitted the discussion of *storge*. One of the problems in our society is the decline of *storge*, which means devotion and loyalty to family, relatives, or a cause. Patriotism and loyalty to one's country or the Church are *storge*. When the Psalms speak of the love of God, they mean *storge* — that is, loyalty and willingness to suffer for His cause. The Jewish religion, especially in ancient times, did not go into flights of fancy about God.

God was seen as absolute. He was approached with fear and trembling, or at least with the greatest reverence. The God who revealed Himself on Mount Sinai was not like God when we visit Him in the Blessed Sacrament. *Storge* also meant loyalty to God and to Israel in the Old Testament. "I have loved, O Lord, the beauty of thy house, and the place where thy glory dwelleth" (Psalm 25:8; Douay-Rheims). It is like the patriotism we knew in the days of World War II, when men and women considered it an honor to risk their lives for their country. Almost every house had a service flag in the window at that time.

Storge also means loyalty to the Church of a kind that does not exist today. In the old days, people of very different views were united in their love for the Church. That has been replaced to an extent by loyalty to persons — a pope, a bishop, a priest. Often personal dynamism determines loyalty today, and in its absence, loyalty to the Church declines. Formerly, it was not like that. Loyalty meant a connectedness and fidelity to the institution, to the Body of Christ, which had little or nothing to do with individual leaders. It was based on love, really on *storge*. If someone did not love the Church, he might get out. One was either in or out.

Storge also applies to family. Before the twentieth century, most marriages everywhere were arranged. The goal was to ensure the continuance of the family, the tribe, the civilization. There were wider interests at stake than those of two individuals. That did not mean that there was no love between the couple or that love could not develop in time. In the twentieth century, with the advent of motion pictures, a more romantic view of marriage and family gained acceptance. Romantic films retold the story of Romeo and Juliet in countless forms, and people were fascinated with the growing idea of friendship in marriage.

Philia

IT IS PREDICTABLE that many relationships between human beings move from *storge* to *philia*. *Philia* is a relationship of mutuality, of friends. Parents became friends to their children. Marriage became a friendship, which resulted in the Christian Family Movement and Marriage Encounter to strengthen the *philia*, or friendship, of marriage. Friendship became the foundation of things, but as we know, friendship comes and goes.

A problem arises in the fact that *storge* lasts forever; *philia* may well not. "Once an Irishman (Englishman, etc.), always an Irishman" sums up *storge*. We cannot change basic characteristics about ourselves, but we can change our friends.

Philia — mutual friendship, the love coming from friendship — may not last. It depends on a person's psychological state and often on external circumstances. When *philia* is the determining factor, marriage or a religious vocation is less stable. People are likely to give up and leave either situation when the going gets tough. That is because *philia* is much less committed than *storge*, and this undermines a lot of our society.

People wonder why there is little commitment today. One reason is that friendship is less predictable than psychological identity, which is linked to *storge*. Young people frequently have no idea of *storge*, of doing something for family or church. Part of the problem is our contemporary philosophy of selfism, which is not good for friendship. Selfism has three principles: my first responsibility is to fulfill all my potential for pleasure and for the fulfillment of my capacities; second, if anyone else's rights stand in the way of my rights, I must put mine first; and third, the world owes it to me to fulfill all my needs. Selfism is the message of every radio and TV program, and it has undermined American life and Western civilization. In fact, it may very well do the republic in, since a democracy or shared government cannot survive long in an atmosphere of selfism.

Selfism makes friendship difficult, if not impossible. Who wants to be the friend of the selfist? In his book *New Rules* (1981), Daniel Yankelovich, a distinguished social scientist, analyzed this and claimed that selfism would dig its own grave, which he predicted would occur by the year 2000. He maintained that the most virulent and damaging symptom of selfism was abortion. In 2006, selfism and abortion are, most regrettably, still very much with us. *Philia* does not have much impact in such an environment. *Storge* is gone, so we are left with *eros*. Fun and fulfillment. And a great deal of American life survives on that. The heroes of American culture are people who lead totally dissolute, egocentric lives — film, rock, and TV stars, whose personal lives are in chaos. Some people are corrupted by money, and a great many others, if they had as much money, could have been corrupted as well.

Agape

THE FOURTH GREEK TERM to describe love is *agape*. It corresponds to the Latin *caritas*. The general word for "love" in Latin is *amor*, which can include everything. *Caritas*, or *agape*, refers to selfless, self-giving love, and it is not often seen in a pure form. In classical Greek, *agape* was used rarely and characterized someone who was willing to die for the city-state in order to preserve the republic, someone whose sense of *storge* pushed them to accept death. The United States once had heroes who said things like "Give me liberty or give me death." People were once honored because they had died for their country. Unfortunately, these things are unlikely to happen today. Rather than seeing *eros* and *agape* as contradictions of each other, Pope Benedict views them as potentially related and even complementary:

> In philosophical and theological debate, these distinctions have often been radicalized to the point of establishing a clear antithesis between them: descending, oblative love — *agape* — would be typically Christian, while on the other hand ascending, possessive or covetous love — *eros* — would be typical of non-Christian, and particularly Greek culture. Were this antithesis to be taken to extremes, the essence of Christianity would be detached from the vital relations fundamental to human existence, and would become a world apart, admirable perhaps, but decisively cut off from the complex fabric of human life. Yet *eros* and *agape* — ascending love and descending love — can never be completely separated. The more the two, in their different aspects, find a proper unity in the one reality of love, the more the true nature of love in general is realized.[49]

The Song of Roland

WE HAVE AN EXAMPLE of *agape* in the medieval epic *The Song of Roland*. After warring for several years with the Muslims of Spain, Charlemagne and his army are returning to France. Leading the rear guard is Roland, Charlemagne's nephew and faithful peer. As they advance through the Pyrenees, they are attacked by the Saracens at the pass of Roncesvalles. Roland has two choices: sound the horn of alarm to bring back Charlemagne's army, or stay and fight, though his few thousand men are greatly outnumbered by the enemy forces. Roland's code of honor — his *agape* — forbids him from summoning the Christian army and exposing them to further danger, so he stands his ground. Though the rear guard is massacred and Roland remains almost alone on the battlefield, he has managed to rout the Muslim army and mortally wound its leader. Before dying himself, he blows the horn, not now in the hope of rescue but that Charlemagne might bury their bodies and avenge their deaths.

In the Gospel, Our Lord tells us, "Greater love has no man than this, that a man lay down his life for his friends" (John 15:13). *Agape* is selfless love. It requires no return. In some cases, as in *The Song of Roland*, it is followed by suffering and death. We admire *agape* in others, but we are less inclined to practice it ourselves, and consequently, it is rare in our society.

Why was Mother Teresa popular? Many people disagreed with her views on nearly every subject, but they admired her enormously because of her selfless generosity. Many religious communities were founded for the purpose of taking care of the poor. They taught and nursed the poor for nothing, and benefactors came to their aid. Gradually, things changed. They became "professional," more upscale. In spite of the founders' intentions, little charity remained.

The human heart admires and responds to charity. Where do we learn this Christian virtue? Perhaps it is learned most effectively through suffering. *Agape* — or love for people with no expectation of return — is a powerful force in the world, but it does not last unless it is carefully nourished. Religious institutes that were begun to teach the poor, now teach the rich. Things that started out being free became costly, and what was intended to be charitable became uncharitable.

Where do we learn this Christian virtue? Perhaps it is learned most effectively through suffering.

Charity is not a perennial. It is an annual. It has to be planted over and over again. Its impermanence is rooted in human self-centeredness and ultimately in original sin. We do not love freely, because we have been hurt so much. We are afraid that if we give something away, we won't get anything back, and we will be nobody. Human beings have three great fears — to be no one, to have no one, to have nothing — and they cause people to be self-centered and ungenerous. We always ask what return we will get for our love. When things fall apart, we become angry with God. We may grow bitter. If we are rejected and everyone turns against us, we soon find out whether we love God.

Agape is the best foundation for Christian marriage and friendship. Saint Augustine says, "Christ loves the Church with *agape*." He gives an interesting example of *agape*. One member of an elderly couple becomes sick, unresponsive, and unaware of self or surroundings. The spouse continues to take loving care of that person. That's *agape*, Augustine says.

Real and False Charity

WHERE DOES LOVE BEGIN? Some people claim to have a universal love for the human race, but they despise many individuals. Cardinal Newman, who had a great gift for friendship, was also very sensitive and got hurt easily. He had this to say about charity:

It is obviously impossible to love all men in any strict and true sense. What is meant by loving all men, is, to feel well-disposed to all men, to be ready to assist them, and to act towards those who come in our way, as if we loved them. We cannot love those about whom we know nothing; except indeed we view them in Christ, as the objects of His Atonement, that is, rather in faith than in love. And love, besides, is a habit, and cannot be attained without actual practice, which on so large a scale is impossible. We see then how absurd it is, when writers (as is the manner of some who slight the Gospel) talk magnificently about loving the whole human race with a comprehensive affection, of being the friends of all mankind, and the like. Such vaunting professions, what do they come to? that such men have certain benevolent feelings towards the world — feelings and nothing more; nothing more than unstable feelings, the mere offspring of an indulged imagination, which exist only when their minds are wrought upon, and are sure to fail them in the hour of need.[50]

How much do we know about feelings? The word itself is a vague idea, and yet *feelings* often substitute for real thought in today's world. Feelings can be good, but they are not a solid basis on which to build our lives. They are like Ivan in *The Brothers Karamazov*. Dostoyevsky makes him the symbol of atheistic humanism. He loves mankind, but individually he hates everyone he has ever known.

Newman continues:

The real love of man must depend on practice, and therefore, must begin by exercising itself on our friends around us, otherwise it will have no existence. By trying to love our relations and friends, by submitting to their wishes, though contrary to our own, by bearing with their infirmities, by overcoming their occasional waywardness by kindness, by dwelling on their excellences, and trying to copy them, thus it is that we form in our hearts that root of charity, which, though small at first, may, like the mustard seed, at last even overshadow the earth.[51]

The Most Important Element

FROM NEWMAN'S ANALYSIS we can conclude that love begins at home or in the workplace. The most important element of all charity is forgiveness.[52] I think we even feel that we must forgive God at times because His providence *appears* to fail us. We have to forgive those we love when they hurt us.

Forgiveness is the indispensable element that makes life together possible — whether it be in a religious community or marriage, or between parents and children or friends. When Christ came into our world doing only good for people — healing the sick, raising the dead to life, feeding the multitudes — their response was to reject Him and make Him undergo a torturous and agonizing death. We need not fool ourselves into thinking that the same thing would not happen today, should He return. In fact, He is often crucified in our midst. Look around.

Charity is not a warm and fuzzy feeling. It must be given to us by God. We cannot earn it; we cannot produce it. If we simply have feelings of benevolence and kindness — the virtue of humanity, according to positive psychology — we are not practicing charity. Benevolence is fine. It may be the foundation of a charitable personality, but it is not charity. Charity is a gift of God, and the only way we can tell whether it rises above the level of natural benevolence is to apply Our Lord's words in the Gospel: "You have heard that it was said, 'You shall love your neighbor and hate your enemy.' But I say to you, Love your enemies and pray for those who persecute you, so that you may be sons of your Father who is in heaven" (Matthew 5:43–45). In doing this, we have to be careful because people sometimes love their enemies so that they themselves can suffer. That is passive aggression, or an unconscious attack on self.

I had an early experience of the love of enemy with my second-grade teacher, Sister Teresa Maria, of the Sisters of Charity. For many decades she taught the second grade, and I'm sure she never lost her temper once.

I became intrigued by the fact that about fifteen minutes after school ended each day, Sister Teresa Maria would go out of the convent carrying a box or a tray covered with a napkin. If it was a cold day, steam would be coming from the tray. Curious, I followed her one day through a busy but poor street and watched her enter a tenement house. The barber we went to happened to be in the basement of that tenement, so the next time I got a haircut, I asked Giuseppe, the barber, what Sister was doing there. He told me that she took care of an old woman on the fourth floor who was quite sick.

More intrigued than ever, I climbed up the fire escape one day to see what it was all about. I climbed up on a milk box by a window and stood absolutely horrified. Looking directly at me through the window was the wicked witch from *Snow White and the Seven Dwarfs*, which I had recently seen. I jumped off the milk box and ran down the fire escape. I hurried up the street and entered the church. In my fear I rushed up to the altar of the Blessed Virgin. I can still see the blue vigil lights; I knelt down to pray because I had seen a witch.

As I was praying, a question came into my mind: "How come the witch did not harm Sister Teresa?" The answer was obvious: Because she was good to the witch. I said to myself, "Maybe if people were nicer to witches, they wouldn't be quite so bad." And suddenly the words came into my mind as clear as a bell: "Be a priest." (Up to that point I had been thinking of being a fireman.) All this was so real to me that when I came out of the church, I glanced over at the rectory, which looked a bit foreboding. I decided then and there that God was calling me to become a priest, although I wasn't too enthusiastic about it.

I told no one of my experience or of my decision to be a priest. One day the following year, my third-grade teacher, Sister Consolata, gave me a holy card, and written on the back were the words: *Ora pro me*. My father asked me why she wrote the phrase in Latin and told me to ask her. Sister said quite directly, "Because you are going to be a priest."

I told the story of my encounter with the "witch" at my first Mass, long after Sister Teresa Maria, who was present, had forgotten the incident. Another member of her community reminisced with me about that time: "Oh yes," she said, "I remember those days. That was Miss Pettit that Sister Teresa Maria took care of. She hated Catholics, and she never referred to Teresa Maria as 'Sister' once, although Sister took care of her for three years until she died."

Sister Teresa Maria had understood and put into practice Our Lord's words: "Love your enemies: do good to them that hate you" (Matthew 5:44; Douay-Rheims).

When we cast bread on the waters (see Ecclesiastes 11:1), it usually comes back to us as wet bread. Not only did Miss Pettit never become a Catholic, but she probably died bitter and thoroughly anti-Catholic. Sometimes, however, the bread we cast has a lasting effect. Sister Teresa Maria's great charity was valid and meritorious of itself, and it also served indirectly to plant in my mind the seed of a vocation to the priesthood. I have never since thought of being anything else.

And all of this happened because an unknown and holy nun performed a hidden act of charity, never realizing that anyone saw her going about on her errand for the poor. It has been said, *Caritas vincit omnia* — "Charity overcomes all."

Questions for Meditation on Charity

1. What are the different types of love described in this chapter and how do they relate to the virtue of charity?
2. How does this virtue embody all other virtues?
3. How does the expectation of no return fit into the *Catechism*'s definition of charity (cited at the beginning of the chapter)?
4. How can we exercise this virtue in our daily lives? Where does charity begin?

Prayer

Heavenly Father, You have created all things out of love. All things proceed from You because of Your love. Your divine Son and the Holy Spirit come from You out of love. All of creation is an expression of Your love, and the salvation of the world by Your divine Son is the accomplishment of Your love. You have first loved us when we did not love You, and You did not cease loving us when we turned away from You to dark things or our own selfishness.

Help us, then, O good Father, to love as we are loved. As we make our way through life, we are aware that we have very little love, that our love wears very thin and often disappears the moment it is challenged. Keep before us the example of Your Son, and by the light of the Holy Spirit call us to love, to overcome evil with love, to persevere in doing good with love, and at the last moment of our lives to surrender to You in love. We pray to You through our Lord Jesus Christ, who lives and reigns with You and the Holy Spirit, one God, forever and ever. Amen.

Afterword

How to Grow in Virtue

THE QUESTION OBVIOUSLY presents itself at the end of this consideration of virtues: How do we live a life that is directed by them? How do we achieve a virtue-driven life?

For more than a half century, psychotherapy, education, and even spiritual direction have been hamstrung by the relativism and determinism of Freud and his followers. Subtle and pervasive passivity and defeatism have led people with difficulties to see themselves simply as victims of life and of what Shakespeare called "the slings and arrows of outrageous fortune."

Now we are summoned by positive psychology to try to change, to adopt positive values, and to develop character strengths and virtues. Hopefully, convinced Christians have been doing this all along, but timidly, even furtively, lest we appear to be naïve about the potentials of human behavior. A whole new approach to pastoral counseling, focused on virtue and character strength, needs to be developed.

How do we tap into the new insights of this exciting time? It is a legitimate expectation that in the coming decades there will be a new thrust in spiritual writing toward the development of character. Let's see what we can do now with some simple but effective steps.

The beginning of all conversion and self-improvement is the recognition that something is either missing or wrong. We hope that the dramatic examples of different virtues included in this work have led readers to see that some of them are absent from their lives or at least in need of renewal and revitalization. Look at your deficiencies, omissions, and habitual failings and sins, and see what is missing. If you are a child of the twentieth century, you may feel it is hopeless to attempt a change. Forget about it. Think of the virtues you are weak or deficient in, or that you do not practice at all. Write them down, along with the character strengths that make up the practice of these virtues. Think of ways to develop them.

For instance, courage is a virtue that makes us reliable in difficult situations and enables us to face discomfort or danger when pursuing and maintaining the truth. You may feel that you lack courage, either altogether or to a degree necessary to confront the challenges of your life. Recognize that you may grow tired of putting up with annoyances or inconveniences. Realize that you may get hurt, passed over, or affronted if you are determined to do what is right. Decide to do what you should — what is right and morally required — even in small matters. As we say in Jersey City, you have to be willing to "pay the two bucks."

All of this can be verified by appropriate Gospel texts in which Our Lord tells His disciples that they will have to suffer for His truth. "They will put you out of the synagogues; indeed, the hour is coming when whoever kills you will think he is offering service to God" (John 16:2). Every day you should examine how much you have cultivated the character strengths that make up courage. Some of these character strengths include patience, endurance, a studied disregard for prejudice or unfounded criticism, and a willingness to speak out against the foolishness of those with sick ideas. When virtue is pursued with courage, one of the rewards is the awareness that God goes with us, that Christ accompanies us.

I know a number of pro-life rescuers who have experienced this presence of Our Lord when they have spent more than a year in prison protesting infanticide, dishonestly called "freedom of choice." Without the awareness of His presence, the terrible injustice of imprisonment would have been a bitter burden, but honesty got them there, and courage strengthened them through their ordeal with joy and confidence.

The Christian Moral Virtues

IT IS ALSO IMPORTANT to identify Christian moral virtues as such. The ultimate goal is to seek first the kingdom of God (see Matthew 6:33). The motivation for natural virtue — the leading of a happy life — is often insufficient to support the actions required. We often see people energetically choosing things, like various addictions, that will only bring them an unhappy life.

Seeking the kingdom of God for oneself or others is often the necessary motive. An example of the two levels of motivation can be seen in the courageous opposition to legalized abortion. Respect for human life should provide a motive for the natural virtue of courage. The awesome respect for the immortal soul of every being, a truth known only by revelation, can provide a more positive motive. The second motive will not eclipse the first, but will give it a greater influence and increase our determination. Pro-abortion political leaders who acknowledge that they personally do not approve of abortion are an excellent case in point.

Helps to a Virtuous Life

THE SIMPLE PROCEDURE outlined above can grow into a profound force if it is followed consistently and if the whole array of virtues and character strengths is practiced. Reading Holy Scripture, especially the Gospel and the whole New Testament, as well as meditating on reliable accounts of the saints' lives, will give you all the necessary cognitive ammunition. Don't sit around like the victimized and deprived disciples of the old negative psychology. Pick up your cross and follow Christ. To use Saint Paul's expression, "Fight the good fight" (1 Timothy 6:12).

A word needs to be said about growing in the theological virtues. Recall that faith, hope, and charity are pure gifts of God. We cannot acquire them ourselves. However, we must receive these gifts and put them into practice. For instance, teaching the truths of faith, applying the truths of faith in everyday life, and intelligently handling the challenges to faith will increase the practice of this virtue. Even doubts can become part of the growth in faith. In *Introduction to Christianity*, Pope Benedict XVI points out that faith in our time may be measured by our willingness to struggle with the doubts generated by materialism and skepticism.

Stay tuned! I expect that the new approach in character and virtue will influence more writings coming from academic psychology and spiritual authors. By the grace of God, the John Paul II generation somehow missed the general illusion that they were victims.[53] They have been cheated in many ways, deprived of good example, given inadequate and even erroneous religious instruction, and poor leadership. Nonetheless, they are a different breed: positive, hopeful, and believing.

I have spent half a lifetime struggling against the tide in psychology, though perhaps not struggling effectively enough. Now as I prepare to fold my tent and move on to eternity (pray for me), I am delighted to see the first signs of a new day for those who really believe in God and truly want to follow His Son, Jesus Christ.

Notes

1. In 1978, as head of the KGB, Andropov contacted his station chief in Warsaw demanding to know how he could have permitted the election of a Polish pope. He was convinced that Americans, particularly Zbigniew Brzezinski (President Carter's national security adviser), and some Europeans were in league to overthrow communism in Poland by engineering the election of a Pole to the papacy. No paranoia there.

2. The following books are recommended: Peter Kreeft, *Back to Virtue* (Ignatius Press, 1992); William Bennett, *The Book of Virtues* (Simon & Schuster, 1993); *The Heart of Newman*, ed. Father Erich Przywara, S.J. (Ignatius Press, 1997); Christopher Peterson and Martin Seligman, *Character Strengths and Virtues: A Handbook and Classification* (Oxford University Press, 2004); Father Andrew Apostoli, C.F.R., *Walk Humbly With Your God: Simple Steps to a Virtuous Life* (Servant Books, 2006).

3. Dr. Alice von Hildebrand, an eminent philosopher I consulted on Kant, points out that he wrote a superb refutation of his own position in his less known work, *Fundamental Principles of the Metaphysics of Morals.*

4. See his autobiography in three volumes: *Particulars of My Life, The Shaping of a Behaviorist,* and, especially, *A Matter of Consequences.* See also *Psychology Today* 17 (September 1983), 22–33.

5. These theories were espoused by, respectively, Alfred Adler, Viktor Frankl, Harry Stack Sullivan, Karen Horney, Conrad Baars, and Abraham Maslow.

6. Paul C. Vitz, "Psychology in Recovery," *First Things* 151 (March 2005), 19.

7. Ibid.

8. Peterson and Seligman, 13.

9. Dietrich von Hildebrand, *Christian Ethics* (New York: McKay, 1953).

10. The *Catechism of the Catholic Church* refers to natural virtues as human virtues (cf. nn. 1803–1804).

11. See. A. Tanqueray, *The Spiritual Life* (Desclée and Co., 1930), 472ff; R. Garrigou-Lagrange, O.P., *Christian Perfection and Contemplation* (Tan Books, 2004).

12. See Andrew Newberg, M.D., et al., *Why God Won't Go Away: Brain Science and the Biology of Belief* (Ballantine Books, 2002).

13. Joseph Cardinal Ratzinger, *Introduction to Christianity* (San Francisco: Ignatius Press, 2004), 49–50 et passim.

14. *De moribus eccl.* 1, 25, 46: *Patrologia Latina* 32, 1330-1331.

15. St. Thomas Aquinas, *Summa Theologiae*, II-II, 47, 2.

16. See David G. Dalin, *The Myth of Hitler's Pope* (Regnery, 2005).

17. See the several books by Sister Margherita Marchione, including *Consensus and Controversy: Defending Pope Pius XII* (Paulist Press, 2002) and *Shepherd of Souls: A Pictorial Life of Pope Pius XII* (Paulist Press, 2003).

18. See *"We Are Your Servants,"* trans. Audrey Fellowes, ed. John E. Rotelle, O.S.A. (Augustinian Press, 1986). This book is no longer in print.

19. J. H. Newman, *University Sermons*. Sermon 10: "Faith and Reason, Contrasted as Habits of Mind," n. 43.

20. Lincoln Barnett, *The Universe and Dr. Einstein*, with introduction by Albert Einstein (New York: William Morrow and Company, 1968), 106.

21. J. H. Newman, *Discourses to Mixed Congregations*, Discourse 13: "Mysteries of Nature and of Grace."

22. J. H. Newman, *Grammar of Assent*, chap. 2: "Revealed Religion."

23. J. H. Newman, *Parochial and Plain Sermons*, IV, Sermon 19: "The Mysteriousness of our Present Being."

24. See Fr. Benedict J. Groeschel, C.F.R., *A Still, Small Voice* (Ignatius Press, 1993).

25. Saint Augustine, *The City of God*, Book XIX, chapter 4.

26. Ibid., chapter 5.

27. Poulenc's opera is based on actual events that befell the Carmelite nuns of Compiègne in 1794, but departs in many points from historical fact. The character of Blanche, for example, a rather contrived attempt to focus dramatic tension, is a complete fiction.

28. J. H. Newman, *Parochial and Plain Sermons*, I, Sermon 6: "The Spiritual Mind."

29. So-called, from the Latin *cardinem* ("hinge"), because the other virtues derive from them. In recent psychological studies cited above, they identify six major virtues and many subdivisions. Essentially the psychological studies are using a more modern classification and do not seem to reflect the uniqueness of theological virtues.

30. For a readable contemporary review of the basic truths of faith, please see my book *Why Do We Believe?* (Our Sunday Visitor, 2005).

31. J. H. Newman, *Discourses to Mixed Congregations* (1849), Discourse 10: "Faith and Private Judgment."

32. Ibid.

33. J. H. Newman, *Discourses to Mixed Congregations*, Discourse 11: "Faith and Doubt."

34. J. H. Newman, *Discourses to Mixed Congregations*, "Faith and Private Judgment."

35. Robert Jastrow, *God and the Astronomers* (New York: W.W. Norton, 1978), 11.

36. J. H. Newman, *Discourses to Mixed Congregations*, Discourse 13: "Mysteries of Nature and of Grace."

37. Pope John Paul II, *Crossing the Threshold of Hope* (New York: Knopf, 1994), 9–11; italics in the original.

38. Ibid., 11.

39. *Let God's Light Shine Forth: The Spiritual Vision of Pope Benedict XVI*, ed. Robert Moynihan (New York: Doubleday, 2005), 94.

40. Pope John Paul II, *Crossing the Threshold of Hope*, 193.

41. J. H. Newman, *Idea of a University*, Discourse 9: "Duties of the Church towards Knowledge."

42. At the end of the ten-month siege, no strategic or tactical advance had been made by either side.

43. Pope John Paul II, *Crossing the Threshold of Hope*, 61.

44. Ibid., 62–63; italics in the original.

45. J. H. Newman, *Twelve Meditations and Intercessions for Good Friday*, #10, "Jesus our Guide and Guardian."

46. Cf. Jn 13:34; italics in the original.

47. Robert D. Enright and Richard P. Fitzgibbons, *Helping Clients Forgive: An Empirical Guide for Resolving Anger and Restoring Hope* (American Psychological Association, 2000), 31. Fitzgibbons has done extensive psychological studies on the process of forgiveness, specifically on forgiveness and *agape*.

48. Pope Benedict XVI, *Deus Caritas Est*, n. 5.

49. Ibid., n. 7.

50. J. H. Newman, *Parochial and Plain Sermons*, II, Sermon 5: "Love of Relations and Friends."

51. Ibid.

52. See Enright and Fitzgibbons for a remarkable and scholarly study of forgiveness therapy.

53. See Kreeft, 191. Several years ago, Kreeft, who is both a perceptive observer of the passing scene and a strong proponent of virtue, saw this trend among the young. Perhaps it is part of healthy youthfulness to be inspired by the challenge of virtue.

Excerpts for Meditation From the Sermon on the Mount

The Beatitudes

Matthew 5:3-12

Blessed are the poor in spirit, for theirs is the kingdom of heaven.

Blessed are those who mourn, for they shall be comforted.

Blessed are the meek, for they shall inherit the earth.

Blessed are those who hunger and thirst for righteousness, for they shall be satisfied.

Blessed are the merciful, for they shall obtain mercy.

Blessed are the pure in heart, for they shall see God.

Blessed are the peacemakers, for they shall be called sons of God.

Blessed are those who are persecuted for righteousness' sake, for theirs is the kingdom of heaven.

Blessed are you when men revile you and persecute you and utter all kinds of evil against you falsely on my account. Rejoice and be glad, for your reward is great in heaven, for so men persecuted the prophets who were before you.

Salt and Light

Matthew 5:13-16

You are the salt of the earth; but if salt has lost its taste, how shall its saltness be restored? It is no longer good for anything except to be thrown out and trodden under foot by men.

You are the light of the world. A city set on a hill cannot be hid. Nor do men light a lamp and put it under a bushel, but on a stand, and it gives light to all in the house.

Let your light so shine before men, that they may see your good works and give glory to your Father who is in heaven.

Love for Enemies

Matthew 5:43-48

You have heard that it was said, "You shall love your neighbor and hate your enemy." But I say to you, Love your enemies and pray for those who persecute you, so that you may be sons of your Father who is in heaven; for he makes his sun rise on the evil and on the good, and sends rain on the just and on the unjust. For if you love those who love you, what reward have you? Do not even the tax collectors do the same? And if you salute only your brethren, what more are you doing than others? Do not even the Gentiles do the same? You, therefore, must be perfect, as your heavenly Father is perfect.

Concerning Almsgiving

Matthew 6:1-4

Beware of practicing your piety before men in order to be seen by them; for then you will have no reward from your Father who is in heaven.

Thus, when you give alms, sound no trumpet before you, as the hypocrites do in the synagogues and in the streets, that they may be praised by men. Truly, I say to you, they have received their reward. But when you give alms, do not let your left hand know what your right hand is doing, so that your alms may be in secret; and your Father who sees in secret will reward you.

Concerning Treasures

Matthew 6:19-21

Do not lay up for yourselves treasures on earth, where moth and rust consume and where thieves break in and steal, but lay up for yourselves treasures in heaven, where neither moth nor rust consumes and where thieves do not break in and steal. For where your treasure is, there will your heart be also.

Do Not Be Anxious

Matthew 6:25-34

Therefore I tell you, do not be anxious about your life, what you shall eat or what you shall drink, nor about your body, what you shall put on. Is not life more than food, and the body more than clothing? Look at the birds of the air: they neither sow nor reap nor gather into barns, and yet your heavenly Father feeds them. Are you not of more value than they? And which of you by being anxious can add one cubit to his span of life? And why are you anxious about clothing? Consider the lilies of the field, how they grow; they neither toil nor spin; yet I tell you, even Solomon in all his glory was not arrayed like one of these. But if God so clothes the grass of the field, which today is alive and tomorrow is thrown into the oven, will he not much more clothe you, O men of little faith? Therefore do not be anxious, saying, "What shall we eat?" or "What shall we drink?" or "What shall we wear?" For the Gentiles seek all these things; and your heavenly Father knows that you need them all. But seek first his kingdom and his righteousness, and all these things shall be yours as well.

Therefore do not be anxious about tomorrow, for tomorrow will be anxious for itself. Let the day's own trouble be sufficient for the day.

Saint Augustine's Prayers for Virtue

In whatever I say, come to my help, O You one God, one true eternal substance, where is no discord, no confusion, no change, no want, no death; where is all harmony, all illumination, all steadfastness, all abundance, all life: where nothing is lacking and nothing redundant: where begetter and begotten are one: God, whom all things serve which do serve and whom every good soul obeys.

At last I love You alone, You alone follow, You alone seek, You alone am I ready to serve: for You alone, by right, are ruler; under Your rule do I wish to be. Command, I pray, and order what You will, but heal and open my ears that I may hear Your commands, heal and open my eyes that I may see Your nod; cast all unsoundness from me that I may recognize You! Tell me whither to direct my gaze that I may look upon You, and I hope that I shall do all things which You command.

O Father, cause me to seek You; let me not stray from the path. As I seek You, let nothing else take Your place! If I desire nothing but You alone, let me find You now. Should any desire remain in me for something other than You, purify me of it, and make me fit to look upon You! For the rest, whatever concerns the welfare of this mortal body of mine, so long as I do not know how it may serve either myself or those I love, I commit it to You, Father, who are wisest and best. I pray that You will correct me whenever necessary. I implore You, O most Merciful One, to convert my inmost self to You; and as I journey to You, let nothing stand in the way. Command that so long as I endure and care for this same body, I may be pure and magnanimous and just and prudent, a perfect lover and learner of Your wisdom, a fit inhabitant of a dwelling place in Your most blessed kingdom (*Soliloquies*, Book I, 4, 5).

How much You have loved us, O good Father, Who have spared not even Your Son, but delivered Him up for us evil people! How You have loved us, for the one who thought it not wrong to be equal with You became obedient even to death on the Cross. He who alone was free among the dead, with power to lay down His life and power to take it up again; for us He was to You both Victor and Victim, and Victor because Victim. For us He was both Priest and Sacrifice, and Priest because Sacrifice: delivering us from slavery to be Your sons, by being Your Son and becoming a slave. Rightly is my hope strong in Him, who is at Your right hand and intercedes for us; otherwise I would despair. For many and great are my infirmities, many and great, but Your medicine is more powerful. We might have thought Your Word remote from union with us and so have despaired of ourselves, if the Word had not been made flesh and dwelt among us (*Confessions*, Book X, 43).

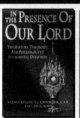
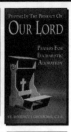

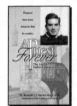